Praise for *Work Better Together*

In order to thrive, we need to put humans first and systems second. Jen Fisher and Anh Phillips give us a path to strengthen work relationships and personal well-being to make productive, innovative, and trusted teams possible.

—**Arianna Huffington,** founder and CEO, Thrive Global

Relationships and values are critical to our ability to flourish in work and life. But how do you bring them into your work in a way that makes a real difference? Jen Fisher and Anh Phillips have the answer: meaningful connection is key to professional fulfillment. In *Work Better Together*, they offer practical advice for creating a workplace culture that puts relationships first.

—**Jonathan Fields,** bestselling author and founder of
   Good Life Project®

The Zulu greeting *Sawubona,* of my native country South Africa, literally means "I see you." *Sawubona* is the emotional theme of *Work Better Together.* In this helpful and timely book, Jen Fisher and Anh Phillips show how to bring our full humanity to work in organizations.

—**Susan David,** PhD, award-winning psychologist and
   bestselling author of *Emotional Agility: Get Unstuck,*
   Embrace Change, and Thrive in Work and Life

High-performing teams don't happen by accident. They are the result of intentional decisions to create strong working relationships, and habits that promote collaboration and individual well-being. In *Work Better Together,* Jen Fisher and Anh Phillips weave two strands of success—strong relationships and individual well-being—into a clear path for teams to follow.

> —**Nataly Kogan,** founder and CEO of Happier, Inc.,
> and author of *Happier Now*

Work Better Together teaches managers how to build trusted teams of belonging, engagement, creativity, and safety. Put those values at the heart of your work rituals, and great performance will follow.

> —**Erica Keswin,** workplace strategist and bestselling
> author of *Bring Your Human to Work* and
> *Rituals Roadmap*

What could be more timely or important than a book about well-being in the workplace? On weekdays most adults spend the bulk of their waking hours at work, either in person or remotely. As Jen Fisher and Anh Phillips explain in *Work Better Together*, 80 percent of us feel we lack close, meaningful relationships with our coworkers, which in turn damages our relationships with our employers and diminishes our effectiveness in the workplace. Their book offers a road map that leaders at all levels of any organization can follow to improve the psychological well-being of their employees, and, ultimately, the efficiency of the organizations they lead.

> —**Adam Alter,** Professor of Marketing and Psychology,
> New York University Stern School of Business and
> *New York Times* bestselling author of *Irresistible* and
> *Drunk Tank Pink*

If you want to change the game, start with your Wolfpack! Jen Fisher and Anh Phillips show how leaders at all levels can support more dynamic teamwork with humanity and purpose. Offering rich insights and simple strategies, *Work Better Together* will be your playbook for creating strong relationships in the workplace.

—**Abby Wambach,** soccer icon and bestselling author of
Wolfpack and *Forward*

The urgent need for organizations to become more human triggers the question *HOW?* How can business drive greater decision making and innovation at the team level? How can that contribute to employee well-being? *Work Better Together* answers those questions with clear guidance for making productivity and well-being mutually reinforcing. Leaders who embrace its advice will reap the rewards in better performance and a more engaged workforce.

—**Erica Volini,** Deloitte Global Human Capital Leader

Jen Fisher and Anh Phillips are visionaries—*Work Better Together* is an inspiring step-by-step field guide for sparking human potential. Our jobs have a profound impact on our physical, mental, and emotional health. Jen and Anh illustrate how humane workplaces—filled with kindness, psychological safety, teamwork, and meaning—allow productivity and innovation to flourish. This book will show you how to make your work more joyful while boosting results.

—**Kelli Harding,** MD, MPH, and bestselling author of
The Rabbit Effect

In the era of virtual work, wellness is no longer a luxury; it's a business and lifestyle necessity. In *Work Better Together*, Jen Fisher and Anh Phillips share insightful and practical advice for creating a positive workplace culture by encouraging positive technology habits, supporting employee well-being, and nurturing human skills.

> —**Amy Blankson,** bestselling author and cofounder,
> Digital Wellness Institute

Whether your team meets virtually or face-to-face, people need to bring their full humanity to every encounter and take as much pride in their leisure as they do in their work. That's the lifeblood of creativity and innovation, and *Work Better Together* prescribes dozens of ways leaders can inspire better performance and better well-being at work.

> —**John Fitch and Max Frenzel,** bestselling coauthors of
> *Time Off*

I believe in the power of peer allies to help people build career endurance. I teach leaders of all ages to strengthen those connections at work, especially in tough times. *Work Better Together* has a plan for that, beginning with determining the principles of strong relationships and continuing on to greater well-being for all.

> —**Joan Kuhl,** author of *Dig Your Heels In* and
> *Misunderstood Millennial Talent*

WORK BETTER
TOGETHER

WORK BETTER
TOGETHER

How to Cultivate Strong
Relationships to Maximize Well-Being
and Boost Bottom Lines

JEN FISHER

ANH PHILLIPS

New York   Chicago   San Francisco   Athens   London
Madrid   Mexico City   Milan   New Delhi
Singapore   Sydney   Toronto

2 3 4 5 6 7 8 9   LCR   26 25 24 23 22 21

ISBN   978-1-264-26812-2
MHID   1-264-26812-2

e-ISBN   978-1-264-26813-9
e-MHID   1-264-26813-0

Library of Congress Cataloging-in-Publication Data

Names: Fisher, Jen (Jennifer), author. | Phillips, Anh Nguyen, author.
Title: Work better together : how to cultivate strong relationships to
   maximize well-being and boost bottom lines / Jen Fisher and Anh Phillips.
Description: New York : McGraw Hill, [2021] | Includes bibliographical
   references and index.
Identifiers: LCCN 2021007451 (print) | LCCN 2021007452 (ebook) |
   ISBN 9781264268122 (hardback) | ISBN 9781264268139 (ebook)
Subjects: LCSH: Interpersonal relations. | Work environment. | Job
   satisfaction. | Well-being.
Classification: LCC HM1106 .F555 2021 (print) | LCC HM1106 (ebook)
   | DDC 302—dc23
LC record available at https://lccn.loc.gov/2021007451
LC ebook record available at https://lccn.loc.gov/2021007452

McGraw Hill books are available at special quantity discounts to use as premiums and sales promotions or for use in corporate training programs. To contact a representative, please visit the Contact Us pages at www.mhprofessional.com.

*To all dolphins current and aspiring—thank you
for reminding us to connect with one another
and to the joyful spirit within each of us.*

CONTENTS

ACKNOWLEDGMENTS

It takes a squad to write a book, and we're incredibly grateful to our squad for their help, encouragement, and support.

This book would not have been possible without the hearts and minds of Doug Hardy and Amy Fields. Thank you for helping us bring our ideas to life and tell our story.

We'd also like to thank Deloitte's Well-being team (Sammy Loh, Mel Anzelc, Jaime Ledesma, Cree Scott) and the Tech Insights research team (Kelly Gaertner, Stefanie Heng, Natalie Martella, Matt Calcagno, Abhijith Ravinutala, Maria Wright) for the impact they make every day. We couldn't ask for more talented and amazing team members to work with! Working with each of you is an honor, and provided inspiration for many of the stories told and lessons learned in this book.

Thank you to Deloitte leadership for your support, particularly retired Deloitte CMO Diana O'Brien, who has been a great mentor and friend. And we want to show our appreciation to Sue Nersessian for her careful review of the manuscript and to McGraw Hill, especially Donya Dickerson, for seeing the potential in our idea.

Finally, we'd like to thank all our family and friends who have supported us through this effort. Thank you for inspiring and encouraging us.

BRINGING OUR WHOLE SELVES TO WORK

If social psychologists invented a global experiment to determine human capacity for surviving paradox, they'd come up with something resembling the modern workplace.

We are more connected than ever, and yet loneliness is epidemic. We are rich in information, but deciding what to do with that information is more difficult than ever. We can achieve more from our desktops than ever, and yet we are physically and mentally exhausted. Our best work is fueled by positive emotions like empathy, creativity, and shared purpose, and yet we measure our worth exclusively in quantitative terms. Our teams are ever more interdependent, and yet we cling to bureaucratic silos and hierarchies that discourage cooperation.

And as we write this book in 2020, in a cruel amplification of our predicament, the interdependence of employees has been battered by the fight against the COVID-19 pandemic. The psychological strain of physically separating from one another is not the least of the pandemic's ill effects.

Long before workplaces went remote or closed, we—Jen and Anh—were already studying the ways in which work technology affects our well-being. Communicating via teleconferencing, improvising work schedules around childcare, supporting employees who were burning out . . . all this was on our radar before 2020. The irony of starting a book about these topics in 2020 is that all the changes that concerned us accelerated, and all the problems we studied were suddenly increased for millions.

The remedies for workplace burnout became even more urgent because of the pandemic. This book is thus about how to begin the process of change right away.

Psychologists have noted that the inability to control a situation, especially when we've *had* control or think we should have control, can create a major source of anxiety. This, in turn, can greatly add to our stress levels.

The good news is that there are things we can do to help take care of our mental health, especially when it comes to dealing with stress and negative emotions. In fact, one of the most important first steps is to focus on those things you can control.

We wrote this to provide information you can put into action to cope with stress and build resilience. We start with you, the individual, and work out in a series of radiating circles to describe steps that will help your team, your organization, and the extended world (customers, community, and society).

As enthusiastic users of technology, we love the innumerable ways it improves our work and our lives. As a well-being expert (Jen) and researcher on digital transformation (Anh), we also know how easily human interaction with technology becomes habitual and even addictive to the point that its benefits are outweighed by the negative consequences.

One of the topics of this book is about making our interaction with technology benefit our individual and collective well-being as much as our productivity. In that sense, it's also about understanding the meaning of work and making conscious trade-offs between the "pain and the gain" in our relationship to technology—and more importantly, our relationships to each other.

We will also focus on the blurring line between personal technology, such as social media, and work technology. They used to be separate in design, purpose, and interaction, but in the past decade or so, people's interactions with their smartphones feel more and more like interaction with work technology.

Making Meaning

The American novelist and philosopher Benjamin Hale observed, "We, and I mean humans, are meaning makers." We seek to find meaning in our daily decisions, actions, and relationships and especially our work.

Thanks to digital work technology, it's easy to connect with people thousands of miles away. Social media also provides us with hundreds—sometimes thousands—of connections outside of work. But how meaningful are those relationships? It's a vital question, because a sense of meaning provides us with the sense that our lives matter. Degrees of meaning differentiate our relationships at work and home.

It's easy for social media to create a false sense of connection, and that's, in part, why we are lonelier today than ever before. More than 40 percent of Americans say they're lonely. And a growing body of research shows this is (quite literally) bad for our health—raising our risk of stroke, heart attack, even dementia.

At the same time, most of us spend more than half of our waking hours, five days a week, at work. The rest is typically spent running errands, preparing meals, (we hope) exercising, and tending to family needs. Thus, the workplace seems like a natural place to begin to solve—or at least lessen—the isolation and feelings of disconnectedness.

But here's the scary reality: only a fifth of employees have a best friend at work.[1] And the current climate in most of our workplaces is only taking away from that even more. Surveys suggest that employee satisfaction and engagement are declining over time. Only about a third of US workers are psychologically committed to their jobs. Trust in organizations and their leadership is also low.

Burnout is on the rise. In a Deloitte survey of the external marketplace, three out of four respondents said they have experienced burnout in their current job, with more than half saying they felt burned out more than once. In that survey, we asked respondents how they deal with their burnout, and 51 percent say they talk to friends or family.[2] It's not much of a leap then to say that human connections can be healing.

Even when we are inclined to change, the way in which we work today can compound the problem. There's the increase in remote work—like telecommuting and gig jobs—both of which typically don't come with regular, repeated person-to-person interaction. Even when those jobs do, the connections are rarely meaningful—how close can you get to someone during a 10-minute car ride?

People who work in an office are more connected, or at least have the potential to be—but sometimes it feels easier to just send an email than it does to walk down the hall for an in-person chat.

Here's another important nugget to know about workplace relationships: while the idle, watercooler catch-up is technically connecting, the type of relationship—as well as with whom—matters, too. It's not just about everyone being on friendly terms or having a forced drink together every now and then at a work mixer. The relationships have to be deeper than that, and ideally with some of the people you work with most often—i.e., your team. You need trust and the feeling that your coworkers genuinely value and care for you.

This book was born of a similar necessity. As coauthors, we have both experienced the power of meaningful relationships in the workplace, and we've also seen what happens when we overlook making those connections. Then, as we dug into the research on meaningful workplace relationships, we noticed the number of studies, surveys, and reports was growing. Each of us has also come—though in different ways—to truly value the workplace relationships we each have. For if it weren't for our "work family," we'd both likely be in different career places.

JEN'S STORY

I remember the moment I realized that meaningful relationships are key to not only being a great colleague, but also being a great manager. It was the day that a member of my team, a team that I had been managing for a few years, came to me and said, "I don't want to work for you anymore." It wasn't the job she was leaving. It wasn't the organization she was leaving. It certainly wasn't the team she was leaving. It was her manager that she wanted to leave—and I was that manager.

It's a jarring moment for managers to learn that they might lose one of their best employees. But to learn that it's because of your management is another thing altogether. It makes you immediately reflect on who you are as a colleague and manager. It also gives rise to the question, "Why didn't I see this coming?" And the answer was simple: I wrongfully assumed that I could expect things from her without asking, checking in, and making time for personal interactions. I just assumed she'd always be there. And I almost paid a very big price for it. Although I wasn't able to keep her on the team, it did give me the opportunity to reframe my management approach so that this incident would never happen again. And today we remain friends. I will always remember that pivotal moment in my own leadership journey. It's a moment that I share often with others as a cautionary tale, and it's what led me here to coauthor this book.

ANH'S STORY

I remember when my daughter was about six or seven, and we went to a family dinner where she would get to spend time with cousins she doesn't often see. She was so excited about sitting at a separate table with her cousins. But when I glanced over to check on her, all the kids were on digital devices, and she sat there next to them bored and sad. On the ride home, I asked her how dinner was. She said that she didn't have fun because most of the kids were playing separate games and just keeping to themselves. Fortunately, that was not the typical interaction (or lack of it) my daughter has with her cousins, but that day stuck with me. It was like a precursor to adult behavior we've all seen in restaurants: a group of adults at dinner, and all of them on their devices. It reminded me of the patterns, habits, and traps we're all falling into and how we are passing those habits to the next generation.

I used to be one of those managers who was nearly solely focused on getting stuff done, being efficient, and making progress. I was constantly driving activities, and I had zero time for what I considered "idle chitchat" like talking about what everyone did over the weekend.

In time, however, I learned that meaningful relationships with team members helped us all to better achieve our goals—the work is easier to complete, and as a team we are more effective and efficient and have fewer miscommunications. What's more, there is more creativity and engagement among us, a better sense of common and shared purpose, and a strong sense of trust and support for each other. We feel more human, and we also have more fun. Reflecting on the 20-plus years of working in various roles (from technology implementation, to project management, to research) through this lens, I realize that the biggest challenges I've seen teams face were rooted in people and relationships, and rarely the technology, the deadlines, or the actual work.

As I became a researcher and started exploring how organizations navigate their way through a digital age, I found that people are often at the center of challenges and successes. In my research on how companies are reinventing themselves in a digital age, most leaders we interviewed said that the technology is the easy part. The harder part is undertaking organizational and cultural change, developing and retaining talent, and being more innovative. And at the heart of these endeavors are ideas and actions performed by people, not machines.

Well-Being as a Foundation for the Workplace

There is another increasingly urgent reason we need more human connection in the workplace. As AI, or artificial intelligence, begins to take over some of our routine repetitive work, the nature of the work that will remain will be highly cognitive, creative, and intellectual. These are the so-called soft skills—the right-brain, subjective, most "human" skills—and they are the skills of the future. Other critical soft skills in greater demand include empathy and emotional intelligence, critical thinking, embracement of change, interpersonal communication skills, and authenticity. Ultimately, acquiring and implementing these skills will make us better at collaborating and will strengthen our human connections in the workplace. They will also enable people to work better with automation and AI in what Deloitte calls the "Age of With"— where the most human qualities partner with the most powerful digital capabilities for optimized outcomes.

But here's the challenge: showing your human self can be scary. We're inclined to stick to the superficial chitchat because it feels safe. Think about a time that you had to share something deeply personal with your boss or with a coworker on your team— "I'm pregnant"; "I'm getting divorced"; "I have cancer"; or "My significant other lost his job." How did you feel in the moments that led up to that disclosure?

Showing our vulnerabilities, or disclosing what feels like too much, makes us worry that we will be seen as weak, less competent, or exposed. We have to move past that worry, because showing our vulnerabilities is one of the keys to having authentic human relationships and building trust. We also have to become more open-minded to others' experience and points of view. Whether that's one-on-one or as a team, our ability to welcome our vulnerabilities *and* our strengths into the workplace will increase our happiness and our effectiveness with one another.

With some intention, a commitment to thinking differently, and an understanding of the benefits, being more human at work is doable. And that is the goal of this book. In the following chapters, we lay out the importance and value of meaningful workplace relationships. Then, based on 40-plus combined years of experience, we supply you with the tools to invest in cultivating true, authentic relationships in your workplace, regardless of who you are or how many people you lead. We don't claim to have all the answers; nor do we imply that we are experts in relationships. We are human and have certainly made many mistakes in the past. But we are passionate about the power of meaningful relationships at work, and we've pulled together our learnings from our research and experiences to share with you.

In the way that companies have really begun to embrace corporate social responsibility and are implementing programs to help improve the physical health of their employees—both of which also financially benefit their bottom line—it's time that organizations and their leaders prioritize their employees' psychological well-being.

Stepping into a New World

A 2020 Deloitte report noted:

> By 2017, as the tensions between humans and technology continued to accelerate, it became clear that an even more radical transformation would be required to enable humans and technology to work productively together. . . . We suggested that organizations needed to "rewrite the rules" to navigate the exponential change that arrived with the full onset of the digital age. Those new rules would require more than merely inserting technologies into existing structures and processes. Instead, organizations needed to think about how to redesign jobs and redesign work in ways that represented a fusion of, rather than a trade-off between, humans and technology. With the recognition that technology, human, and business issues are not separate but intertwined came the realization that these issues would have to be approached in new ways.[3]

At Deloitte, we and our colleagues believe that the task of redesigning jobs and work emphatically includes designing well-being in the flow of work. This was evident long before the pandemic emergency of 2020, because the forces working against well-being have been growing for decades.

We cannot predict the course of the global pandemic. Perhaps by the time you read these words, the disease and economic havoc it caused will be behind us. But the pandemic did not cause the workplace problems we'll examine here. It focused our message and reinforced the urgency of the need to change.

History is not linear. Its cycles and breakthroughs, its unintended consequences and unrealized currents, all humiliate most predictions. As we review the economic and business predictions based on pre-2020 data, we're reminded that black swan events make interpretation of trends very difficult. The COVID-19 pandemic raises questions that could resolve in completely different directions. For example:

- As economies recover and people go back to work, will the labor market snap back to pre-2020 low unemployment rates, or will businesses, reserving cash for another rainy day (or a return of epidemic conditions), be reluctant to hire?
- Will economies grow their way out of recession quickly and at a steady pace, or will continued/renewed shutdowns create a regionally and industry-specific asymmetric recovery? For example, will hospitality, sports, and entertainment businesses lag manufacturing, construction, and professional services?
- Will 2020 permanently change the workplace? Will remote work be the new normal? How will mass virtual work impact human interaction and organizational culture? What will this do to well-being as the boundary between work and home blurs? What will it do to our relationships at work?

We hope that however the economic and business story of the next two to five years plays out, the better impulses that so many of us found in the pandemic remain. We hope the workplace can foster a renewed spirit of community and cooperation and mutual respect. This will only happen if we find the courage to transcend the attitudes and habits that brought us here.

We—and by that we mean the two of us and you, all of you—can expand the idea of well-being to embrace the physical, mental, financial, and spiritual health of anyone in that community we call the workplace.

Crises and longer disruptions demand innovation for the simple reason that what worked yesterday isn't working today. This happens during wars (massive industrial innovation), pandemics (medical breakthroughs), and economic and political crises (such as the Great Depression) as well as cultural turning points (the civil rights and women's movements). Innovation will continue in technology, medicine, and manufacturing and also in business models and ways of doing business: public-private partnerships; government use of universities as laboratories of invention; sustainability and clean energy investment and technologies; and the movements to make workplaces more diverse, inclusive, and psychologically safe.

Becoming more human at work, and nurturing the best in our relationships, is the next great innovation.

PART ONE

OUR CRITICAL CONNECTIONS

People live within a dynamic web of connections. At work, at home, in the community, and wherever else we go, our relationships with other people shape how our lives are spent, interacting with our unique qualities like skills, temperament, values, and knowledge. It's easy to take these connections for granted, and yet unless we are aware of the qualities of those connections, and make deliberate choices about them, we can be swept along in a tide of unconscious habits that don't reflect our truest selves. When that happens, our most valued work and most important relationships never reach their full potential. Part One consists of three chapters that explore these ideas.

Chapter 1 reviews the ways in which our habituation to technology at work and home is subtly undermining the purpose of having technology in the first place—that is, to make our lives better, more productive, and more attuned to our work and personal values. The connection between our original intent and our current relationship to technology needs resetting, or our own well-being will continue to suffer.

In Chapter 2, we'll show how connection to other people is essential to mental and physical health. Relationships based on trust create meaning. Strong relationships prevent burnout and bolster engagement at work, and we need to build better connections.

Chapter 3 calls on us to rethink our connections, to become more aware of their different qualities, and to move from a reactive to a mindful relationship with both people and technology.

CHAPTER 1

THE GREAT DISCONNECT

We used to work with our hands for many centuries;
then we worked with our heads, and now we're going to
have to work with our hearts, because there's one thing
machines cannot, do not, and never will have, and that's a
heart. I think we're going from hands to heads to hearts.

—Tom Friedman

Ellen* is a senior executive at a global firm. She manages more than 200 technical and professional people, who work in cross-disciplinary teams at several locations. She has high expectations of herself and her teams. Ellen prides herself on practicing the best management techniques, and she delivers: year over year,

---

* Ellen is a fictional compilation of many executives we have observed. Full names indicate real people who agreed to share their stories and insights with us.

her teams are rated among the most accomplished in the company. She takes a hands-off approach, acting as a coach, mentor, and strategic thinker and avoiding micromanagement. And she uses the latest business technologies to do her work; throughout the day she's on email, teleconference apps, and her smartphone. At any moment, she might switch from answering urgent requests, to setting a check-in on her calendar, to writing a note of congratulations to her niece, who earned academic honors this semester. There are days when Ellen's mind seems like an extension of all the technologies she uses to stay in touch.

And yet Ellen has long had a nagging feeling that she is somehow becoming less connected to her team, her work, and even her friends. The endless activity online assumes a life of its own—she can't help checking messages even when she's on the phone. While she studies a report or proposal, some part of Ellen's mind is still turning over her to-do list for the day. More and more, Ellen notices that 10 or 20 minutes have passed focusing on some low-priority task, as if she just needed a break from the intensity of the minute-to-minute information processing and communication that make up her 50-hour workweek.

Once she notices her distractedness, Ellen sees it in everyone around her, from her team to her fellow executives. What was once a deliberate consideration of ideas is now a fast search for the data point that would enable a quick decision. What was once social interaction, in calls or in person, has become a kind of information tennis match, with everyone volleying ideas, data, questions, requests, comments, greetings, opinions, and anything else that comes to mind . . . nonstop throughout the day.

The situation isn't much different after work hours. In fact, there are fewer hours that are truly walled off from work. Ellen habitually checks emails on her phone "one last time" before bedtime. Lately, she tries to observe a "no electronics after 8 p.m." rule, only to break it and add disappointment in herself to her never-ending list of stressors. Nobody told Ellen she should never stop working—in fact, her company recommends that people not work 24/7. But the stream of emails, messages, and information never stops, and always threatens to overwhelm her and everyone else.

Ellen and her colleagues are caught in a paradox—more connected than ever but actually connecting less. And several colleagues have confided to Ellen that, while they are performing more activities and even hitting all their performance goals, they share her sense that they are less insightful, creative, or accomplished these days. "We talk about network congestion when there's so much demand for information that our computer networks slow down," says Ellen. "That's how I feel some days."

If Ellen's situation sounds familiar to yours, it's because this is becoming a common picture. We have steadily progressed toward a tech-heavy, information-overloaded, 24/7 workplace culture. From email communication to videoconferencing, it feels (literally) like our networks are congested. Even worse, the incoming workforce lacks essential soft skills, which is very much a result of our tech-focused lives. In short, since the industrial age, we have adopted more, and more, and more technology, but many of us haven't adapted all that well to it. Now we're facing the downstream impact: we are overloaded with data and activity, but we have lost meaningful human connection, particularly in the workplace.

The Mania for Efficiency

In 1911, engineer Frederick Winslow Taylor published *The Principles of Scientific Management.* It was the first modern study of work, aggregating a lifetime's ideas about how any work can be measured and made more efficient. Taylor advocated "scientific" analysis to determine how much work a "first-class" worker could do in a day and to identify the best employee for every job. He believed that planning departments staffed by clerks could map out everyone's work in advance, moving employees "very much as chessmen are moved on a chess-board." Even as he stressed the need to overcome people's "natural laziness," he also wrote, "If the workman fails to do his task, some competent teacher should be sent to show him exactly how his work can best be done, to guide, help, and to encourage him, and, at the same time to study his possibilities as a workman."[1]

We might recoil in horror at such mechanistic views of human employees, but Taylor's outlook reflected his time, when increasing efficiency in every business (think railroads, steel mills, sewing machines, telephones, electric lighting) was generating unimagined wealth and new possibilities for material security—at least for those fortunate enough to share in the gains.

Though Taylor's methods are obsolete, his urgent search for efficiency in every working endeavor still permeates our work cultures. We still want to do more, produce more, accomplish more. Our management methods are more humane, but our most successful businesses and technologies still emphasize efficiency—though we might call it "frictionless commerce" (online shopping) or "instant satisfaction" (video streaming) or even "curated experience" (news aggregators).

Now we work on digital platforms that provide tremendous efficiencies by acquiring and distributing information at the speed of light. Software teams around the globe code so that an application is continuously built, tested, refined, and deployed. Warehouse systems receive orders, command robots to pick and package items, and maintain inventory while humans supervise the processing of information. Oil rigs pass information on their output to hubs that balance demand and delivery. Office teams continuously update each other on every kind of knowledge work. And every activity, by human or robot or information processor, is continuously monitored and observed against the urge to become more efficient.

This "digital Taylorism" is embedded in daily work even in the most advanced and prestigious jobs. While the 40-hour workweek was enacted into law in 1940, it reflected the physical stresses of laboring in factories and fields and applied to hourly workers, requiring overtime pay for more than 40 hours of work. But salaried workers are exempt from overtime rules and generally expected, by both company policy and social pressure, to work as long as it takes to achieve goals.[2]

This is the lifestyle we call "workism": eat lunch at your desk; work late; bring work home; check email before bed and on the weekend. It's a formula for actually working a 50-, 60-, or even 80-hour workweek. At the top of the economic pyramid, in Silicon Valley and Wall Street and the glass towers of America's business districts, working long hours is a badge of honor.[3]

Many people can work a long week for a limited time, but studies show that chronic overwork doesn't result in greater output, because after a certain amount of work time (it varies by person), productivity declines.[4] And in the long run, stress-related health problems such as depression, diabetes, heart disease, and sleep disorders have a huge impact on productivity.[5]

The average knowledge worker receives more than 100 emails a day.[6] We learn new applications and new features, trying to manage the workload, inadvertently adding even more activity. Knowledge workers are interrupted 50 to 60 times a day.[7] Many communication apps adopt a timeline or newsfeed interface— a continuous stream of call-and-response. If "notifications" are turned on, a flag jumps into view or a smartwatch buzzes, setting off a Pavlovian urge to check out the new information. Dan Lyons, author of *Lab Rats: How Silicon Valley Made Work Miserable for the Rest of Us*, cites a familiar scenario: "You have the tyranny of [this app] on your computer all day long, and it's constantly popping up. You're trying to work, and you feel compelled to answer. You get nothing done because you're constantly trying to stay on top of this . . . conversation or multiple conversations."[8]

What about multitasking? In the sense of concentrating on several tasks at once, there is no such thing. Research psychologists use the term "task switching" for behaviors like reading an email while talking on the phone and scanning a timeline. The continuous shifting of attention hurts productivity by cramming a number of partially done tasks into one short period of time. Rapid task switching can reduce productivity by as much as 40 percent.[9] Multitasking at work is about as "efficient" as texting while driving, and there's a reason that's illegal in 48 states.[10]

It takes about 23 minutes to get back on task after an interruption, and somewhere deep in our workism-trained psyche we sense it. People react to interruption by working harder and longer, resulting in elevated levels of stress, frustration, workload, effort, and pressure.[11]

The theme of doing more in less time is a quiet drumbeat underneath so many company cultures that we hardly notice it. And the promise of efficiency and productivity is part of the pleasure we feel when we discover a new technology that helps us do more . . . or at least appear to do more. Answering an email, responding to a message, learning a new bit of information—all can feel like really accomplishing work. Our brains get that little shot of dopamine, similar to the habit-forming pleasures of social media. And we become habituated to the information torrent so that it becomes our cognitive "new normal," proceeding faster and faster. Only that little nagging sense that we used to get more done in less time interrupts the pleasurable flow of call-and-response.

Innovation, Empathy, Humanity, and . . . Technology

While efficiency helps productivity, getting caught in a never-ending search to do more and more is actually damaging our ability to focus on the human capabilities that are most valuable in the knowledge economy.

As efficiency was a key tool of the twentieth-century industrial economy, the twenty-first-century knowledge economy requires innovation, empathy, creativity, collaboration, leadership, and emotional intelligence. Business journals burst with urgent suggestions for bringing these subjective talents to our workday. In a globalized and heavily digitized world economy, the growth of a business relies on innovation—producing a product or service that is qualitatively better than what's out there. Innovation happens when diverse populations—all kinds of minds—work together to imagine new solutions to problems or create new business opportunities. Disruptive technologies like cloud computing and artificial intelligence power innovation in ways barely imagined just a few years ago.[12]

"Economies are shifting from an age of production to an age of imagination," notes a Deloitte report. "In the past, business success relied mainly on deploying precisely calibrated skills to efficiently construct products or deliver services at scale. Today, success increasingly depends on innovation, entrepreneurship, and other forms of creativity that rely not just on skills, but also on less quantifiable capabilities such as critical thinking, emotional intelligence, and collaboration."[13]

Over the centuries, work has evolved from primarily agricultural to industrial to knowledge work. During the agricultural and industrial ages, people worked primarily with their hands, doing physical labor. In the second half of the twentieth century, that shifted more to knowledge work, stereotyped by the nine-to-five desk job. But today the nature of work is shifting again, requiring an elevated level of mental performance to solve problems and come up with new ideas—and with that a new need for softer skills of communication, creativity, empathy, and emotional intelligence. As Tom Friedman describes it, we are shifting from working primarily with our hands, to our heads, and now to our hearts.[14]

A balance of technical skills and social skills distinguishes many jobs at the high end of compensation, prestige, and organizational power. For example, as algorithms take over much of the quantitative work of financial analysis, financial managers need strong social skills to talk with customers, investigate their needs, and design custom investment plans. Management analysts still need to conceptualize abstract ideas and create spreadsheets, but they also need to understand company culture, habits, and social dynamics. Systems researchers and computer engineers, obviously gifted in math, need strong communication skills in order to connect with the business problems they're trying to solve as well as manage teams in today's agile development environment.[15]

Even the most quantitative, fact-based jobs are demanding more and more soft skills. A review of job postings for data science and analysis jobs showed greater demand for creativity, teamwork, problem solving, and even writing than the average of all jobs. More and more jobs are requiring a combination of left-brain and right-brain skills—sometimes referred to as hybrid skills.[16]

The job market is dynamic. Different skills become more valued as the business environment changes. As robots and algorithms take over routine tasks (and entire jobs), people have to shift to different types of work requiring creativity, collaboration, emotional intelligence, and connection.

We are just in the middle stages of a transformation. AI lacks emotional capabilities . . . for the moment. A new set of AI technologies called "affective computing" is attempting to help computers better "understand" humans and to correlate events with human emotions or emotional factors.[17] How will we respond if our technology becomes "emotionally intelligent"? Will we become even more deeply embedded in the demands of our work tools, or be liberated by them? And how steep will this learning curve become as technology more closely resembles real people?

For some the prospect of learning a new set of skills is exciting, but for many the new world of ever-changing job requirements is threatening. The biggest obstacle to success in a transforming work environment might be ourselves. Pressure to perform mounts at the same time that requirements and goals change. A Deloitte study of these changes noted that "with any disruptive transition, we tend to experience fear and stress, generating an impulse to hold on to what has driven success in the past. We must resist that temptation and use the shifts in the nature of work and employment as an opportunity to achieve more of our potential."[18]

The Health Consequences

Because we've adopted technology faster than we've adapted to it, we're paying the price with our physical, mental, and emotional health.

Caught up in the shiny promise of new technologies, and also facing an ever-changing demand for skills, we struggle to keep up. The 2020 Edelman Trust Barometer found that more than 60 percent of people surveyed believe that the pace of change in technology is too fast.[19]

It's more than the speed of change—it's that the change is still accelerating. "Over the past two to three decades, the pace of technological progress and the speed of its diffusion across countries have been startling," noted an OECD report in 2019. "For instance, while it took over seven decades for phone penetration to go from 10% to 90% in US households, it took only about fifteen years for mobile phones and just over 8 years for smartphones. Such technological leaps have had major impacts on the way people work and live."[20]

Is the 24/7 workplace culture making us incredibly productive? No. In fact, the inexorable ramping up of attention time is making people *less* productive. And it certainly is making them more anxious, less happy, less healthy, and less engaged at work. The consequences of trying to keep up include sleep deprivation and fatigue, stress and depression, strains on family and community life, and the shortchanging of the other responsibilities and pleasures of life.[21]

To understand why this is, think of the type-A workaholic who shuns sleep for work time. Chronic lack of sleep undermines ordinary cognitive and motor functions. A University of Pennsylvania study found, for example, that people who got only four to six hours of sleep a night for two weeks showed cognitive impairments comparable to going entirely without sleep for three days.[22] Amazon's Jeff Bezos suggests the consequences aren't limited to one person's health. He said, "Making a small number of key decisions well is more important than making a large number of decisions. If you shortchange your sleep, you might get a couple of extra 'productive' hours, but that productivity might be an illusion. When you're talking about decisions and interactions, quality is usually more important than quantity."[23]

And sleep deprivation is hardly the only problem. Scores of studies associate chronic overwork with depression, anxiety, hypertension, chronic fatigue, heart attack, and increased alcohol consumption.[24]

Heavy use of social media has a variable effect. Studies show that people who perceive their online interactions as negative are more prone to depression and anxiety than people who perceive them as positive.[25]

During the COVID-19 pandemic in 2020, many office workers relied on teleconferencing applications to continue working from home. So much time in screen-based meetings caused physical and cognitive stresses. Interacting on-screen reduces the brain's ability to read multiple unconscious cues, such as a person drawing breath before speaking or leaning forward. And watching many people interact on a single screen (or talking over one another) challenges the brain to decode a jumble of unfamiliar signals. No wonder we all complained about exhaustion after a day spent in telemeetings.[26]

In short, business leaders and employees have focused so intently on efficiency, productivity, and technology that most of us are in danger of burning out. While there may be short-term performance gains, it is not sustainable in the long term, and well-being will suffer. Furthermore, organizations that are simply competing on productivity and efficiency will likely be left behind in an age of disruption and innovation. Companies need to rely on their people for creativity, innovation, problem solving, and collaboration—drawing heavily on cognitive and emotional capabilities that can't perform optimally without well-being.

The system needs an upgrade. We'll show the human and business reasons for making that upgrade in the next chapter.

KEY POINTS

- The drive for efficiency has characterized business for generations, but it no longer guarantees success in an age when innovation is key to navigating disruption.
- People use business technologies to become ever-more productive, often to the point of becoming *less* productive.
- The physical and mental toll of the ever-increasing use of work technology strains today's most important work skills, like empathy, communication, and focus.

CHAPTER 2

WHY WE NEED CONNECTION

> I define connection as the energy that exists between
> people when they feel seen, heard, valued; when they
> can give and receive without judgment; and when they
> derive sustenance and strength from the relationship.
>
> —Dr. Brené Brown

Today we're the most technologically connected we've ever been. The integration of technology into our work and personal lives has happened faster than almost any other disruption in human history. And as a result, we are just starting to see some of the impacts that technology has on our lives.

Internet-based communication technology carries a lot of benefits: It allows you to easily connect with someone on the other side of the world, or stay in touch with childhood friends, and even makes it so that you can almost effortlessly work with someone thousands of miles away. But despite all these possibilities, our constant connectedness has the potential to draw down two key resources—our time and attention. Technology also plays a role in blurring the line between work and life,[1] contributing to that "always-on" feeling.[2]

Technology is inherently neither good nor bad. Like any tool, it depends on how it's used.

Historian Yuval Noah Harari describes one of the psychological changes that technology has brought to our emotions and our consciousness: "Humans have bodies. During the last century technology has been distancing us from our bodies. We have been losing our ability to pay attention to what we smell and taste. Instead we are absorbed in our smartphones and computers. We are more interested in what is happening in cyberspace than in what is happening down the street. If something exciting happens, the gut instinct of social media users is to pull out their smartphones, take a picture, post it online, and wait for the 'likes.' In the process they barely notice what they themselves feel. Indeed, what they feel is increasingly determined by the online reactions."[3]

As our technology use has skyrocketed, loneliness has simultaneously risen. In fact, rates of loneliness have doubled since the 1980s. Chronic loneliness can shorten your life as much as smoking 15 cigarettes a day can.[4] Other research suggests that loneliness can significantly raise your risk of having a heart attack or stroke.[5]

Our work environment has also shifted greatly in recent decades—we are deconstructing work and focusing on the fastest and most efficient ways to get things done. Telecommuting and flextime are also much more common, and the "gig economy" has exploded. The benefit is that these changes now afford us flexibility. The drawback, however, is that these shifts have also reduced opportunities for in-person interaction. Less human interaction is problematic because, by nature, people have a basic human need for social interaction and purpose—and not just in our personal lives, but also through our work and workplace. So now we have inadvertently propagated a culture that has removed humanity from the workplace. The workplace, however, is where we spend between a third and half of our waking hours each week.

Let that sink in for a minute. We have diminished the social connectedness in a place where we devote a very significant amount of our time in our lives. And we've done it in more ways than one.

Work and Psychological Safety

Psychological safety is a feeling of confidence that you won't be treated in ways that harm your emotional, mental, or spiritual self. It has huge implications for the workplace. Safety means you offer ideas and employ your skills without constantly looking over your shoulder, fearing that you will be criticized or punished in some way. Safety means you can make mistakes and learn from them— what we might call the importance of being bad at something— without disproportionate negative consequences.

A key attribute of such safety is the ability to share emotions. For example, someone who is taking on a difficult project can express feeling both excited for the opportunity and apprehensive about failure. In a safe environment, teams and managers respond with acceptance (and might share stories of times they felt that combination of emotions). Sharing feelings, and understanding they are accepted, normalizes those feelings and builds trust.

Reams of research prove that a psychologically safe environment is more productive than one that relies only on rewards like money or position. As Harvard Business School professor Amy C. Edmondson notes, the traditional culture of "fitting in" and "going along" spells doom in the knowledge economy. Success requires a continuous influx of new ideas, new challenges, and critical thought, and the interpersonal climate must not suppress, silence, ridicule, or intimidate.[6]

When people fear speaking up, the work suffers. Innovation suffers. Trust falters. People don't see themselves as being part of a team because they might have a different point of view from the majority. When people fear speaking up, listening also suffers, not only because group pressure discourages debate and analysis of new ideas, but also because people afraid for their psychological safety spend a lot of mental energy, attention, and analysis protecting themselves.

It's obvious that a hostile work environment, whether that's created by a bad boss or a toxic culture, kills psychological safety. What is less obvious is that our subtly learned culture of workism also kills psychological safety. Think of meeting a colleague in the hall or online:

"Hey, how are you doing?"

"I'm so crazy busy, I don't even have time to eat."

"Me too. I'm so busy, I'll never catch up. I'm gonna work this weekend just to get my emails under control."

Does this conversation sound familiar? Even when people commiserate about being overwhelmed, the workism culture treats it like a badge of honor. We think, "I'm proving my value to the company by being overworked." If we're used to processing 200 emails a day, we get anxious on the day when only 20 come in ("Only a couple emails . . . *What's wrong?*") We don't treat a quiet day as an opportunity to disconnect or get a bit of recovery. It becomes a day to catch up on all the unimportant tasks. And before we know it, we're writing another to-do list.

The point is, they are still unimportant tasks. We could be shifting our minds to more important tasks, or more restorative behaviors. Too often, however, we reach for the habituated behavior to reestablish the feeling that we are really, really busy, and therefore *valuable*.

The onslaught of social media and work messaging might mean we never even differentiate between important and trivial tasks because we're immersed in a continuous stream of stimulus coming at us so fast that we don't have time to consider each on the merits. We slip into a workism zone of consciousness: stimulus and response. If you've ever looked up from your collaboration feeds and realized, to your surprise, that 40 minutes have passed since your impulsive urge to send just one message, you can identify with this cycle.

The employee who is always overwhelmed, but also valuable, comes to associate feeling stressed with feeling valued. Parts of life that used to matter, like community or hobbies or interests outside of work, or even physical health, get less time than they used to. Or more insidiously, they become more items on more to-do lists that never really get our full attention. The culture of workism, in which never doing enough to be satisfied is a badge of honor, soaks into a person's psyche; and soon enough, every activity becomes an opportunity for more self-criticism and more burnout.

Dr. Tessa West, associate professor of psychology at New York University, reports in the *Wall Street Journal* that this even drives employees to lie, to their own detriment. She writes, "As pressure to work untenable work schedules rises, employees feel that their survival forces them to lie about using policies designed to improve work-life balance. That means working during time off, such as taking business calls during a child's soccer game or working during paternity leave."[7]

How does this happen? Not all at once and not always because of negative pressure. There are many rewards to a life defined by the jobs we have, the titles we possess, and the number of emails we process. Money, power, position, a sense of achievement, a sense of mission—all those are material and psychological rewards.

But we can easily start out focusing on tasks done for what they accomplish and slip into a focus on tasks done simply because they are there. See the email and answer it, over and over. Work and busyness become a habitual way of being in the world.

When we depart from the steady stream of emails and messages and interruptions, we can feel a little uncomfortable. It's not always conscious, but our hyperstimulated brains want another little hit of that satisfaction that says, "Okay, got that one done!" Without that, our minds tend toward a low-level anxiety, searching around for more of that satisfying feeling. And the fastest, least challenging way to get rid of that anxiety—momentarily—is to return to the email, the newsfeed, or the message string.

Team leaders can encourage an unspoken workism when they drive for outcomes without acknowledging that there can be different paths to the same goal.

ANH'S STORY: MAKING TIME FOR PEOPLE

I spent the first half of my career serving our clients, often traveling to another city to work at the client site with my project teams. For four to five days a week, my teammates were also my carpool, my dinner companions, and my workout buddies. Socializing and building relationships were incorporated into how we worked, and it resulted in amazing friendships I still keep today.

However, when I shifted out of client service and started working on internal projects in remote teams, every meeting, every interaction, became focused only on driving single-mindedly toward the group's goals. I was determined to prove that we were productive, especially since we were working from home. If I took time out to have a real human conversation with a colleague, I would have this nagging feeling that I wasn't focused on the work. I would get on the phone and have my very long list of things that I needed to accomplish.

I would have told you then that I didn't have time for socializing. I didn't realize how important simple human conversation and contact are for working well together, as it had always been baked into my previous projects and work. Over time, I learned that being 100 percent focused on tasks wasn't good for anyone. It wasn't good for building relationships and trust with my team. It wasn't good, because I didn't know what was going on with people in terms of their personal lives. In retrospect, it not only made me harder to work with; it also made it harder to enable my team to work at its full potential. And being in a situation where opportunities to be social and build relationships weren't conveniently built in, I realized I had to create space for those moments and actively nurture them.

The Cost of Burnout

That connectedness and a sense of community can also prevent burnout, which is on the rise. Burnout is more than your typical stress. It leaves you feeling utterly depleted and impacts most, or all, aspects of your life: you lose sleep, eat poorly, don't exercise, and even may disconnect from relationships.

Our culture drives us to expect perfection (of ourselves and others), although none of us is perfect and we live in an imperfect world. Compounding the problem is the 24/7 nature of technology and how our culture glorifies being busy. Think about it: How many times have you asked people how they are and they've responded, "Busy"? Then they will often go on to justify their response by adding, "Busy is good for business."

When you look at it through this lens, perhaps it isn't so surprising that burnout is reaching epidemic levels across the United States. Studies find that as many as two-thirds of employees experience burnout on the job at some point.[8] Its costs are so dire that in 2019 the World Health Organization deemed burnout an official medical diagnosis.[9] You'd think that being passionate about your work would give you a leg up, but surprisingly, research suggests it could actually make you more likely to burn out.[10]

Burnout creates direct and indirect costs to business. Gallup's research notes that employees who experience burnout are 63 percent more likely to take a sick day and 23 percent more likely to visit an emergency room—which translates into lost productivity and higher healthcare costs. They are also half as likely to discuss how to approach performance goals with their manager, are 13 percent less confident in their performance, and are 2.6 times as likely to leave their employer.[11] Gallup also notes this problem is getting worse as workplace demographics change: 45 percent of millennial employees say they sometimes feel burned out at work, and 28 percent claim they feel *frequently or constantly* burned out.[12]

The Cost of Loneliness and Disconnection

Over 40 percent of Americans today say that they feel lonely. Experts believe the real number is actually even higher. As Vivek H. Murthy, surgeon general of the United States, recounts from his first term as America's chief medical authority: "I met factory workers, doctors, small business owners, and teachers who described feeling alone in their work. . . . During my years caring for patients, the most common pathology I saw was not heart disease or diabetes; it was loneliness."[13]

Murthy spelled out the human and economic costs of loneliness in the *Harvard Business Review*: "It is associated with greater risk of cardiovascular disease, dementia, depression and anxiety. At work, loneliness reduces task performance, limits creativity, and impairs other aspects of executive function such as reasoning and decision making." He defines loneliness as the subjective feeling of having inadequate social connections.[14]

Health service company Cigna released the findings of a study of loneliness in the workplace in January 2020. Cigna's president and CEO David M. Cordani summarized its conclusions: "The trends shaping how we work—increasing use of technology, more telecommuting and the always-on work culture—are leaving Americans more stressed, less rested, spending more time on social media, and less time with friends and family. For the business community, it is resulting in less engagement, less productivity and lower retention levels."[15]

Biologically, we evolved to be social creatures. Fostering relationships and collaborating increased our chances of having a stable food supply and afforded us additional protection from predators. Now that biological need is built into our nervous system, so when we're lonely, it creates stress in our body. A little bit of stress is okay, even good for us (it motivates us to accomplish new goals, pushes us to complete tasks, and can keep us excited about life). But when loneliness persists, chronic stress sets in, and that continuous presence of the stress hormone cortisol can wreak havoc on your body (see sidebar "Stress and Health").

The natural "fix" then is social connection, yes? But the power of it is quite surprising. Turns out, the number one predictor of long-term health is the strength of close relationships, according to research conducted on the Blue Zones (regions of the world where people live much longer than the average).[16] Strong connections and the belief that one has a life of meaning are indicators of a longer life span, resilience over disease and stress, and overall higher quality of life. Based on these findings, Blue Zone researchers concluded that tending to our relationships is a form of self-care. There's other research that shows a single hour of social time improves your odds of having a good day.[17] Each additional hour (up to about six hours) bolsters your odds. The researchers concluded that, in contrast, loneliness and lack of social connection are strong predictors of a shorter and less healthy life.[18]

The Harvard Study of Adult Development, begun in 1938 and still ongoing, has gathered a wide range of data on the mental and physical health of hundreds of people. It concluded that close relationships, more than money or fame, are critical to mental and physical health, happiness, and longevity. The study's current director, Dr. Robert Waldinger, explained in a popular TED Talk: "When we gathered together everything we knew about them at age 50, it wasn't their middle-age cholesterol levels that predicted how they were going to grow old. It was how satisfied they were in their relationships. The people who were the most satisfied in their relationships at age 50 were the healthiest at age 80."[19]

Why then—at least from a public health standpoint—haven't we put as much effort on strengthening human connections as we have on curbing tobacco use? Part of the problem is that it isn't clear whose responsibility it is to address the problem. Our government and healthcare system play a role in helping us to understand the damage that a lack of social connection and relationships causes and the repercussions if loneliness persists in such epidemic proportions. But the most natural place to begin to solve loneliness is where we spend the majority of our time—the workplace. Not only can companies encourage change within their organization, but they can inspire other businesses and organizations to tackle loneliness, and ultimately that ripple effect is how we will drive change at the societal level.

If organizational change feels overwhelming, know this: modeling a workplace culture that encourages connection is more important than implementing any one program. Other small steps can make a significant difference, too. For example, consider helping a coworker. Giving and receiving help is one of the easiest and most tangible ways to build human connection. Plus, this act of kindness will perpetuate positivity, and that positivity will help your brain perform better: 31 percent more productive, in fact.[20]

Dr. Murthy and others have designed ways for people to forge stronger social connections at work, which we'll discuss in Chapter 6.

Stress and Health

Stress stokes cortisol, and cortisol stokes inflammation in your body. In the short term this is just part of life, but long-term inflammation is problematic. That's because it is the tip of the chronic illness and disease iceberg: constant higher levels of inflammation can raise your risk of heart disease, diabetes, obesity, and premature death. There are various steps you can take to quell inflammation and promote a longer life: eat a healthy diet—those good-for-you fruits, vegetables, and whole grains deliver compounds that have the potential to dial down that flame; be physically active regularly; and sleep the recommended seven to nine hours most nights. All these lifestyle changes will help you, and don't forget the most valuable of them all—healthy, strong, close relationships.

Human Disconnection Hurts Business

According to a study of 30,000 employees at 500 companies, over one-third of respondents who said they were the most satisfied with their work also had the strongest social connections at work.[21] In a separate study, they found that people with the strongest connections at work were 40 percent less likely to die of heart disease.[22]

There's a data-gathering practice called "organizational network analysis" that measures the effect of strong and weak ties among people in a group. Over a couple of decades, we've learned that positive social connections in the workplace are critical in improving innovation and creativity. They increase the flow of communication and encourage rapid adoption of new technologies, work methods, or other organizational changes.

People with friends at work find their jobs more satisfying. They're much more resilient to the stressors of the daily workplace and then, quite frankly, of daily life. Considering that we spend a third to half of our waking hours in any given week at work, the workplace is a critical place for developing these meaningful connections that we all need to thrive. We know that social connections at work increase people's commitment to their work, their commitment to their colleagues, and this certainly has a positive impact on the bottom line.

As we move to this more technologically enabled work environment where we're looking at deconstructing people's work and figuring out the fastest and most efficient way to get things done, the urgent question is, are we inadvertently removing humanity from the workplace?

Having strong social connections at work isn't just about giving your employees those feel-good fuzzies. It is also good for business. After food and shelter, belonging is a fundamental need. Yet according to a joint survey by Pew and the American Life Project, only 19 percent of people have a significant relationship with a workmate. A Gallup study found another harsh truth—that 50 percent of Americans have left a job at some point in their career to "get away from their manager."[23] Workplace relationships also help employees with stress and illness. When workers feel they have high-stress jobs, their companies report having markedly high healthcare expenses.[24] But employees with human connections at work say they feel less affected by stress, and they're also less likely to be sick or injured.

Research shows that social connection in the workplace improves employees' commitment to their work and their colleagues. This is incredibly valuable when you consider that the nature of our work is more collaborative today than ever before. Time spent collaborating at work has risen by 50 percent over the past two decades, and so when you have to collaborate a lot, it's that much more important for employees to feel connected and committed to their colleagues.[25]

If you happen to prefer a little "professional distance," don't worry—there is good news. Turns out, workplaces can feel friendly—even if there aren't real friendships—when values like vulnerability, authenticity, and compassion are emphasized. Put another way, the benefit of humanity in the workplace is less directly related to the degree or intensity of the friendship and instead comes from true human connection.

In sum, meaningful relationships at work buffer folks during stressful situations, can cut down on sick time, and fuel on-the-job performance—all of which are tangible business benefits.

How an organization builds and fosters relationships is important, too—and traditional methods don't always work. For example, many organizations and leaders try to build connection with social or networking events or team-building activities. But these aren't always successful—work gatherings don't always promote meaningful connection. Turns out, people don't actually mix at mixers.

Another hindrance is how companies build their organization and staff their departments. Employees are recruited and hired based mostly on individual skills and past successes, and less on the kind of skills that propagate workplace connections. Many companies also utilize an annual performance management system that fosters competition instead of collaboration, rewarding employees for their individual accomplishments and even pitting them against their peers in evaluations.

What if we instead rewarded and promoted people for how they make others around them better, not just for their individual accomplishments? (There is actually precedence for this in the sports industry! Professional basketball, hockey, and soccer teams—they don't just count goals; they also track assists.)

So, despite our need for human connection, what's holding us back?

Trust and Engagement

Our lack of trust is a significant hinderance. In one global survey, 15 percent of professionals said they place "very little" or "no trust at all" in their employers.[26]

At the same time, trust in institutions of all kinds is deteriorating. Before the COVID-19 pandemic, business in general was more trusted than government or media, but 80 percent of those surveyed said they still fear losing their job. In 2020, just before the pandemic, 43 percent of Americans believed they and their families would be better off in five years' time—a seven-point drop from 2019.[27] Among millennials (born 1983–1994), only 26 percent globally thought the economic situations in their countries would improve in the coming year. And the sentiment was worse in the developed economies, where only 18 percent thought things would be better in 2020.[28] (Again, this is data gathered *before* the pandemic shut down the global economy. During the early months of the pandemic, people globally gave more trust in government; historically these quick increases in trust are followed by a quick decline.)[29]

Two of the top five reasons reported for their distrust was a lack of strong senior leadership and the organization not fostering a collaborative environment. This survey also found that trust is missing between employees and bosses: only 49 percent of full-timers said they had "a great deal of trust" in those working above and alongside them. Trust is a major work asset. It fosters efficiency. It aids communication and encourages risk taking. Trust helps keep employees from looking for other jobs, and it produces work that is creative and of high quality.[30]

Employee engagement is also quite low. Gallup found that in 2019, the percentage of workers who were highly enthusiastic and committed to their workplace was only 35 percent. Actively disengaged workers reached 13 percent. And 52 percent of workers were categorized as not engaged; that is, they put in their time but were psychologically unattached to work or workplace.[31]

Employees who would be engaged want three broad things: to feel purpose and meaning from their work, to be known for what makes them unique, and to have good relationships (particularly with managers). Through many years of researching engagement, Gallup has found that the manager or team leader alone accounts for 70 percent of the variance between engaged and nonengaged employees.[32]

Again, when people feel that their colleagues genuinely value and care about them, that's when they feel connected and engaged and able to deliver their best work. Martin Luther King, Jr., put it so eloquently when he said, "Whatever affects one directly, affects all indirectly." Although his commentary was not meant to address meaningful workplace relationships, the sentiment is still relevant and poignant. Now is the time for companies and leaders (at all levels) to encourage human connection in the workplace—and not just for today's workforce, but also for the next generation.

Online and Gig Work

Two ways of working need special focus when we look at the problem of disconnection: online work and gig work. They are rapidly growing and represent unique challenges.

Both of us have worked from home for a long time. Our team members are located in many places around the country, and as a global consulting organization, Deloitte has gone a long way to make remote work an efficient and agile part of the business. Since we've worked virtually for years, we had already thought about many of its particular challenges when the COVID-19 pandemic hit in 2020, and millions more people began working from home.

While we were used to working remotely, the pandemic-induced massive shift from in-person to remote work brought with it changes in behaviors and norms, including a large increase in video calls, often making it a default in our organization and in others. The unfamiliarity of working with a bunch of talking heads on their computer screens is disconcerting for many people new to it. It takes time to get used to scanning all the faces and to learn to communicate without body language and wait to hear the network latency–delayed voices. People learned to share screens, mute themselves, and use a background filter so nobody is distracted by their roommate's yoga routine. They learned to raise hands and take turns sharing information.

Then, as people mastered the quirks of teleworking, we saw more habits creeping into work that are very similar to the habits we mentioned earlier about social media. People are tempted by multitasking, scrolling through email or to-do lists when not talking. Social media feeds on the phone prompt them to break attention away. Objects in the home office—an open book, a pet strolling through—are further distractions. And then they remember they're in a meeting and attention snaps back to the meeting.

This isn't laziness—it's habituation. Much of our screen time *feels* like time alone, because that's how it is most of the time. Making the transition from looking at a screen for information, to looking at a screen for interaction, requires a deliberate shift in outlook. We have to switch from consuming information privately to sharing and building communication with others.

And for many people there are acute difficulties to this new routine. A colleague of Anh's, Tracey Parry, is a widowed single mom. She has a five-year-old at home, and during the COVID-19 pandemic, daycare centers were closed for months. Her daughter needed a ton of attention from the only person in her life at the time, and the mom had almost no time or outlets for adult interaction.

Here's how Tracey tells the story:

> I'm a single mom of a 5-year-old, and most of my family lives far away. During the pandemic I was isolated from my family and felt very alone. But at work, I felt so supported, embraced. People I didn't even feel that close to reached out. Our group has done a great job, and our leaders have been more open, and even kinder, than ever during this time. It means a lot to me that many of our interactions are on camera and people can participate and weigh in. During the first few weeks, videoconferences were solace to me. I was able to be honest about my challenges with no negative repercussions. I was able to be on video with my daughter, Annabelle. I was able to talk about the terrible fires all around us here in California, and about lighter moments like Annabelle raiding food at all hours, or her first day back at school.
>
> I miss the people, the events, the travel, seeing people in person. I started journaling in April about "the year that wasn't."

Everyone recognized Tracey's situation right away and stepped in to accommodate her needs, offering empathy, flexibility, professional and emotional support, and periodic check-ins outside of meetings.

How this massive shift from face-to-face interaction to virtual interaction will play out is not fully knowable. At the time of this writing, few predict that the workplace will look the same after the pandemic ebbs.

But we who have practiced distance collaboration can lend our experience to make our teams more effective, even when technology and habit make it harder. (We'll detail the best ways to work as a team in Parts Two and Three.)

Gig economy workers are among the loneliest across the board. The Cigna study found that 75 percent of them "always or sometimes feel that people are around them but not with them."[33] That means the Uber driver or freelance copywriter might interact with people all the time, and yet three-quarters of the time they feel disconnected. It's no surprise that jobs where interaction is essentially transactional leave little room for relationship building. Although it constitutes a small part of the workforce today (16 percent, though estimates vary), the sector is growing rapidly, especially if you include short-term and temporary workers, who are classified differently from the new generation of on-call workers.

Gig workers often rely on digital technology, and many (like those who provide ride-hailing services) encounter new forms of technology-based stress. For example, the platforms they use are designed for the maximum efficiency we discussed in Chapter 1. While they can in principle choose their work hours, they must accommodate external forces—think commuting time for drivers or office time for remote workers. Video and other monitoring enable the people who control their platforms to track their work and "productivity" by whatever standards they choose. Smartphones track their location, and algorithms give potential clients an unlimited choice of workers to employ, encouraging a cost-quality competition that tends to drive down pay.[34]

Gig workers are subject to what we might call structural loneliness at work. They have no continuity with a team of colleagues that is similar to traditional employees. They aren't formally included in organizational initiatives to combat disconnection. Like managing the rest of their work lives, managing loneliness at work will come down to individual actions. And if disconnection is an inevitable part of their jobs, gig workers will have to strengthen their ties to community outside the realm of work.

For employees who are part of a larger organization, there are many ways to increase connection whether working remotely or together. It won't happen if we continue the relationships we have with technology and each other; the next steps for building better connections are the subject of Chapter 3.

KEY POINTS

- The biggest challenges we face relate to people and people's relationships within the team, which are key to a sense of meaning.
- Burnout, loneliness, and disconnection are on the rise.
- At the same time, trust and engagement are suffering.

CHAPTER 3

WELL-BEING IS THE WAY

> Work can be a powerful force, but only
> when it is continuously curated in a way
> that optimizes human potential.
>
> —Erica Volini[1]

We've seen that burnout, loneliness, low trust, and disconnection at work are the negative consequences of trying to keep up with relentless change, torrents of information, and ubiquitous technology. But they are only inevitable if people continue to approach a new situation with old habits. When employees, managers, and leaders change their way of doing business, they can ride the wave of technological change while consciously choosing a healthier path, one that leads to greater well-being *and* better performance.

In technology we call a quick, temporary solution to a problem a "hotfix"—a little patch of computer code to fix a flaw in a software program. The equivalent in our management of ourselves and employees is to add a bit of change around the edges: an employee assistance program, a gym membership deal, or even a bit more technology (wellness software!). Those are all helpful, but they aren't sufficient to address the negative consequences of the systems we've built over the years.

The lasting solution only happens when people fundamentally change their mindset about how humans engage with each other and with the technologies they use. In this chapter, we'll preview a path to doing that and provide details through the rest of the book.

Because technology and the global business environment are constantly evolving, our outlook must be one of constant evolution as well. There is no end state at which a group can say, "All the problems are fixed, and we'll just keep on as we are now." Your outlook also has to be constantly evolving, your ideas have to be constantly growing, and even many of your work values have to be constantly evolving and growing.

The spring of 2020 brought a dramatic example of reaching the point of crisis and illustrates what we mean by fundamental change.

The COVID-19 pandemic forced those businesses that could operate with most of their offices closed to do so. Frontline and service workers, from medical care to food delivery, had to learn extraordinary precautions, and they had to do it with blinding speed. People had to change activities like shopping or holding meetings or schooling children overnight.

We saw many people change with ingenuity and compassion. As the worst worldwide pandemic in more than a century, COVID-19 forced changes and reinvention of systems because the alternative to change was literally fatal. The changes weren't uniform around the world, but in thousands of businesses, as Microsoft CEO Satya Nadella noted, "We've seen two years' worth of digital transformation in two months."[2]

When things get tough, we tend to fall back on old habits or less-than-ideal behaviors, just to get through. In the spring of 2020, we didn't have that choice. We *had* to change, and the pandemic proved that our capacity to change, as individuals and organizations, is greater than we imagined. Now that we know we have that capacity, we need to summon the courage and imagination to evolve our work cultures and habits for the better.

A familiar illustration of this point is how people improve their physical health. If you make a sudden change (like going on a strict diet for a month), you'll lose weight, but chances are you'll gain it back quickly. If you undertake to change unhealthy habits (say, eating junk food) slowly by substituting healthy habits (switching to fresh fruit and vegetables for snacks and rewarding yourself occasionally), you're more likely to achieve a permanent change. The same program tends to work with exercise, stress reduction, and other well-being programs; they succeed because they are about changing your lifestyle one step at a time, until new habits take over.

Organizations fall into the same trap. They address deep-seated problems with a reorganization or a new focus statement ("Well-being is critical!"), hoping the latest initiative hotfix will raise employee engagement or job satisfaction. Cultural change doesn't happen that way, however. While leaders must decide, articulate, and model organizational changes, the new behaviors and attitudes can only be permanent when they happen in thousands or millions of individual decisions and behaviors. That means a lot of people are going to have uncomfortable moments as they replace old habits with new ones.

To make well-being part of daily work life, we have to raise our understanding of how good intentions are swept away by many different attitudes and behaviors. One is workism. If we measure our worth as employees by how stressed and busy we are, we'll keep pursuing overwork and overstress, even if it doesn't make a measurable, relevant difference in productivity or outcomes. On the other hand, what if everyone had a clear vision of what well-being means, and had the tools and methods and time to achieve it? When long-term well-being is culturally as important as long-term productivity, people will embrace it.

People ignore well-intentioned initiatives due to fear, doubt, or cynicism. Often they embrace the concept of changing toward a healthy workplace culture, but only for another employee or another group. We've seen situations in which people are fully bought into change as an idea, but their behavior says otherwise.

There's ample proof that well-being supports organizational performance for individuals and teams. The challenge that organizations face is creating a wide-ranging set of behaviors that act on individuals and also raise the well-being of the organization as a whole. And the key to success is expanding the focus from bolt-on programs that treat stress and change like a first-aid kit treats an injury, to designing well-being into the flow of work itself.[3]

The Problem with a Reactive Life

Our relationship to digital technology is a bit like our relationship with food: it's necessary to get through the (work)day, but it's easy to slip into mindless consumption (also known as doom scrolling). Jonathan Fields, author of *How to Live a Good Life,* refers to this as part of "Reactive Life Syndrome." In a Deloitte *WorkWell* podcast, he stated:

> Technology has led us to become hyperaddicted to what other people feel is important for us to pay attention to, which creates less and less room in our own lives to be intentional and to choose where to focus our energy. Instead, we constantly react to other people's agendas, other people's

photo streams on Instagram or whatever app we may be using. And when you bundle through a really high rate of input and stimulation with addiction to technology, our brains get the same dopamine hit that they get through drugs when you feel a vibration in your pocket. In fact, simply knowing there's a phone in your pocket, research now tells us, massively distracts you from a conversation, for example. Leaving it on a table is even worse. Our brain is subconsciously thinking, it's been almost 90 seconds; something good must be happening on my phone right now. So it's constantly other people [who] were feeding us what they feel is important in their lives and what they want us to see, so we react to that and react and react and react."[4]

Adam Alter, author of *Irresistible: The Rise of Addictive Technology and the Business of Keeping Us Hooked,* points out that the technology on which we rely daily is deliberately designed to be addictive as well as productive, gobbling more and more of our attention during the day. Our attention is finite, and how much we can give depends on our health, motivation, schedule, stress, and other factors.

It's as if each of us starts the day with an "attention bank account," and we draw it down throughout the day. If screens take more of our attention, we have less to give to coworkers, family, community, and even ourselves. We can refill that account with healthy habits and redistribute how we spend it down. But the addictive attraction of technology is hard to break; it takes conscious effort and even a little discomfort.

The qualities that make technology addictive also highlight a strength in our interaction with technology at work. The digital disruption that Satya Nadella observed is not about technology alone but really about people, who show incredible capacity to adopt new technology and new work habits when they experience the benefit directly. That's why the best designers of business systems look to consumer software these days. Technology that is clearly focused on preserving the status quo of a bureaucracy doesn't inspire anyone but bureaucrats.

As Anh and her coauthors noted in *The Technology Fallacy,* "Employees have become increasingly frustrated by the gap between what they are capable of accomplishing with technology in their personal lives and what they can get done at work when they are limited to email and nonmobile computing."[5]

Moving from Addicts to Advocates

Workism and technology addiction feed each other, and the results are declining well-being and lost potential. How can we move from habitual, reactive behaviors that drain us as employees and humans to healthy relationships with work and work technology?

As technological capabilities continue to advance and the work that people do continues to evolve, leaders will have to prioritize an environment and culture that fosters meaningful relationships among coworkers. There are incredible benefits to cultivating workplace relationships. Research shows that positive practices and relationships in the workplace increase job satisfaction, leading to greater engagement and higher productivity.[6] We're going to show you how to achieve this in your organization.

The remaining chapters of this book provide a step-by-step field guide to decoding your workplace relationships, making healthy decisions about technology in your life inside and outside of work, navigating the increasingly overlapping real and virtual workplaces, and leading healthy change. The key is a renewed focus on our most human qualities by establishing consciously positive relationships with self, tech, and team, starting with our immediate teams and working our way outward to the furthest reaches of the organization and beyond; redesigning work systems and technology habits to put people first; and building well-being into the design of work.

Part Two, "Decoding Your Work Relationships," will lead you to see your workplace relationships clearly and take actions that improve those relationships based on understanding others and yourself more consciously.

Part Three, "People First, Systems Second," will show how you can make your team and yourself more productive with better well-being habits, as well as a mindful navigation of real and virtual workplaces.

Before we go into detail, here are some high-level principles that guide our recommendations.

Rethinking What "Connected" Means

Change begins with awareness of yourself and your surroundings. How well do you understand your relationships at each level? And how accurate is your picture of each person on the team? When you understand why you react to certain people and situations the way you do, rather than acting out of assumptions and habit, you take the power to change into your own hands. We will suggest simple metaphors based in deep research to craft an accurate understanding of what's going on in your team, department, or organization—and how to improve it.

The primary role of teams, from generating innovative ideas to getting things done, is not a new concept. Even the image of a lone genius working into the night on inspiration and raw talent is mostly myth. Leonardo da Vinci had a studio filled with assistants and students. Thomas A. Edison had a whole laboratory of associates (they tried at least 3,000 models of an incandescent lightbulb before finding a successful design).[7] The great engineering feats of the twentieth century were accomplished by innovations in how work got done, and innovations in industrial organization that changed how teams shared information, made decisions, and communicated.

Research shows that teams are truly effective when they operate as more than a collection of talented individuals. Creativity is amplified when people bounce ideas off each other not only in a structured way but in "creative collisions" that happen spontaneously in the social setting of work. This is a dynamic that is hard to bring to videoconferencing, in part because our mind processes information differently on screens—we don't see body language; gestures and timing are different; and because we're sitting in different rooms, our minds register different distractions. Teleconferencing and videoconferencing both limit the group of people with whom we interact, and research shows that unexpected encounters, like conversations over lunch or in an atrium or common area, really feed creativity.

In the twenty-first century, a set of management methodologies evolved that emphasized both how teams worked together and how they worked with other teams in an organization. The best known of these is called "agile," which started in software development and now is applied everywhere. Agile changed development from a "waterfall" model—in which a team slowly creates the best product it can before passing it onto the next team in the production chain—to an iterative model of fast, repeating cycles. Now teams develop a "minimal viable product"—the smallest, fastest working component they can—and then get it to the next group, or even to customers, to get their reaction and then take it back to revise the design based on the feedback. Agile expands the idea of "team" beyond your immediate group to include the people reacting to your product. It has proved superior to old methods in all kinds of product development, from manufacturing to online financial services.

This fast-iteration way of building things changes the organization. It knocks down organizational silos. It compels departments that used to work separately to work together on a project basis. On any project, you might have a development team, a marketing team, a financial team, a supply-chain team, and others all reacting to each iteration of a "minimal viable product" and updating their reaction and their part of the complete picture. People realize that they are, in fact, "all in this together"—not just out of the generosity of their hearts but because that's how they succeed. They understand what they're trying to work toward, and each member is motivated to work with everyone else and figure out how to achieve the common goal.

Thus, work is becoming more collaborative, and organizations are adopting a new culture of constant interaction among a network of teams throughout a product's creation. Then the teams reconfigure around the next project depending on its particular needs, not the org chart drawing. This trend toward constant collaboration is only going to increase in enterprises around the world. It didn't stop during the COVID-19 pandemic; if anything, we saw a greater focus on collaboration and cooperation and adaptation. These are aided by technology, but they are made possible by relationships—trusted networks between people and their teams, and among different teams around the enterprise and around the world, driven by a common purpose.

Internal collaboration tools are designed to share information and also to encourage connections across the org chart, so a person in marketing can find the right person in finance and the right person in product development to get the information needed just at the time it's needed.

Creating healthy teams in the digital age is like creating successful new business ideas. Deloitte's research shows that digital transformations depend on the human experience. Andy Main, former global head of Deloitte Digital and principal at Deloitte Consulting LLP, says this is "a path that circles around the customer, by first connecting to key moments in people's lives, and then shaping experiences and the business around them."[8]

Humans are emotional, messy, and fickle. They are also more responsive to experience than words or ideas. The poet Maya Angelou famously said, "People might forget what you said or did, but they won't forget how you made them feel." If you make your business interactions all about creating a positive experience, people will learn to trust you and depend on you, even if they can't recall the details of how you interacted six months ago.

A real-life example: We've each been on teams where we were the newest person to join (many of you reading this will relate). The others have been working together for a while, and they all know and trust each other, and they've all grown used to their interactions. At first, even a welcoming team doesn't know quite how to trust the new person. The people on the team have (usually unspoken) questions: "Is this new person going to compete with me or promote my interests?" "Will this person share information or hoard it?" "How is this person going to use my ideas, and how should I work best with this person?"

Often (ideally) a new person in the group establishes connections by contributing to the team with all the skills the person can share. The new person listens and promotes the team's success first, confident that his or her personal success isn't threatened by promoting others, sharing information, and earning the team's trust. The new person doesn't have to conform or leave his or her opinions at the door; the healthiest teams welcome diversity of thought and understand it's key to innovative and insightful work.

The business imperative to create trusted teams has finally caught up with the human need to connect with others that we discussed in Chapter 2. Creating healthy connections is too important to be left to first impressions, conformity, workplace politics, or luck. In Part Two, we'll show you how to choose high-value behaviors and systems and identify those "junk food" interactions that might provide a quick hit of ego satisfaction but don't build healthy relationships. We'll also discuss ways to build bridges across differences and overcome barriers that prevent teams from working well.

People First, Systems Second

Part Three of this book shows how to put "people first, systems second." A legacy of twentieth-century management ideas is that people work best when they conform to systems: organizational systems, management systems, data systems, and behavioral systems. Systems in this sense are templates for getting things done by performing an established series of tasks in an established order, and constantly refining the templates so the outcomes are predictable and repeatable. Older management systems are excellent for this purpose; the ultimate systems example from the 1980s was a quality-control methodology called Six Sigma, which dramatically limited defects in manufacturing and other processes, raising quality.[9]

Systems still play an essential role in business, but the world of fast innovation and constant adaptation requires a lot more of that messy, emotional, relationship-based work. Things are going to change, and that is stressful on human beings. When faced with the stress of change, people can turn to endurance (absorbing the change and "toughing it out") or resilience.

The trouble with endurance is that you spend your physical, emotional, and intellectual energy without restoring it. To adapt to changing conditions without burning out, teams need resilience more than they need endurance.

What is resilience? Psychologist Emiliya Zhivotovskaya, a leader in the field of positive psychology and the science of flourishing, says it's a set of skills that anyone can learn: "The simplest definition of resilience is the ability to bounce back from life set-backs, or from challenges and adversities. If you get a cold [and care for it] you will bounce back stronger. If you break a bone, it will come back stronger. Our body knows how to do this, and the kind of recovery that many people need is not actually from major life traumas, it is from day-to-day stresses that we actually need to learn resilience skills for."[10]

We'll show how to develop resilience skills as an individual in Chapters 7 and 8, but it's not up to the individual alone. We've learned that resilience is tied to the support you have around you in terms of your immediate team and your organizational culture. Managing change in business is a group effort; managing change well is key to organizational resilience.

In 2020, Anh worked with colleagues inside and outside of Deloitte to study how organizations were coping with the pandemic crisis, and "resilience" was a term that leaders kept mentioning. They said organizational resilience started with having a strong mission and purpose (beyond survival) around which everyone could unite. That sense of purpose had to be ingrained into the organization long before the crisis, to give people a common focus and reason to change their behaviors, to help one another cope and improvise new ways of accomplishing work.

Organizational resilience also means teams must learn to adapt to changing conditions quickly. Digital disruption means an entire industry can face existential threat in a very short time. Those who focus on endurance, trying to tough out the disruption without changing their business at the core, are simply left behind (the advent of ride-hailing apps cut the cost of a New York City taxi medallion by 90 percent in a few years).[11] Those who adapt to a new world by finding new ways to make money, offering new products or superior service, survive and shape their future. Often the key to adaptability from a digital disruption is digital adaptation, with new skills applied to new business models.

Individual and organizational resilience should work in a self-sustaining cycle that meets change with adaptation; that supports individual needs and group dynamics; that builds adaptability as a central feature of work. The radiating circles of influence feed and support each other. In the resilient organization, the whole really is greater than the sum of its individual parts.

Designing Well-Being into the Flow of Work

Constant change is not going to go away. Disruption is built into the structure of business, and the benefits of efficiency and innovation are too great to ignore. That means we're faced with three options for adapting tech, team, and self to the new normal: endure the stress of change by toughing it out, work to the breaking point and then take steps to recover from the damage, or bring well-being into the flow of work itself.

The first option is too costly whether you look at it in dollar terms (declining efficiency, high workforce turnover, high healthcare costs, low morale) or human terms (too much stress is at the root of great unhappiness—depression, disengagement, dependency, and isolation). The second option dooms people to an unending roller coaster of psychic and physical injury and recovery.

Bringing well-being into the flow of work itself, option three, is the most promising way to deal with all the new pressures of the modern workplace. It requires a thorough rethinking of the ways in which our work routines damage the high-value skills toward which work is trending—creativity, empathy, imagination, communication, trustworthiness, caring. It requires human resources professionals, well-being specialists, and leadership to have the courage to change long-established routines and hierarchies. It requires individuals, from the most senior to the most junior employees, to raise their consciousness of when and where their own routines are damaging their well-being and the well-being, effectiveness, and productivity of their teams.

No long ago, people who promoted well-being ran into obstacles from two sides: Executives demanded a sound business rationale for redesigning established routines. Less senior employees liked the idea of well-being but wanted to know that this was something the organization really supported, so that if people changed their way of working, they wouldn't be impacted negatively. They wanted permission from leadership, their team members, and even themselves, for example, to set boundaries like "No email after 6 p.m." and stick to them without their image, performance review, or advancement opportunities declining.

The methodology called "design thinking" offers a principle where we can begin. Design thinking begins with a focus on what's desirable from a human point of view. Then it uses research to discover what people need, generates many ideas to fulfill that need, builds rough prototypes (including actions and routines), and gets feedback. Finally, design thinking returns to the source, crafting a human story to inspire others.[12]

To bring well-being into daily work, we ask, "How can we design individual and team goals, work styles, and technology so that they create well-being as well as business goals?" Chapters 7 to 10 explore how to do this in the overlapping areas of tech, team, and self. You'll find research, techniques, and stories of how others are designing well-being into work, adjusting the method to the individual needs of every person, organization, or situation.

Designing well-being into the flow of work is a complex challenge, because people are complex individuals. Jobs are complex (and getting more so). Technology grows ever more complex. And organizations, especially large ones, are both complex and hard to change.

But this is also a joyful challenge, because as we increase well-being, we increase human happiness and meaning through our work lives. Instead of burning out our most precious resource—the time we have on this earth—we nurture and promote our most cherished values. Shouldn't work accomplish that?

KEY POINTS

- Turning the workplace toward sustainable positive cultures means fundamental change; and the events of 2020 proved that our capacity for change is bigger than we thought.
- It starts by reframing what we mean by connected—using technology as a means, not an end—with an understanding of our workplace relationships.
- The goal is to design well-being into work for individuals, teams, and organizations.

PART TWO

DECODING YOUR WORK RELATIONSHIPS

Improving the work relationships among self, tech, and team begins with sharpening your awareness of where you are today. Because people are unique, and organizations are complex, that means learning about the work styles of each member of your team as well as your own preferences. Then commit yourself to work habits that respect the differences among people while staying productive.

Long ago, when work was predictable and slow to change, and work relationships were based on strict codes of behavior, you could say, "Just tell me what to do and I'll do it." Those days are over. Now you must be alert to an ever-changing mix of temperaments, cultural expectations, behaviors, and work methods (including technology use).

Chapters 4, 5, and 6 invite you to reflect on what your best work style is, what your current team relationships are, and how to maximize work relationships and individual well-being.

Not all work relationships are destined to be fully satisfying. You can't be best friends with everyone, but you can learn to cultivate meaningful relationships at work with almost anyone. Really learning about yourself and colleagues and being honest about the myths that drive so much of our unexamined work habits—that's the way to ride the waves of change.

CHAPTER 4

WHAT'S YOUR WORKPLACE STYLE?

Chemistry is a huge factor in business. And not just in established working relationships, but in any interaction between people, whether they know each other well or not. Once you start looking, its presence or absence is noticeable everywhere.

—Kim Christfort and Suzanne Vickberg,
Business Chemistry

Consider these three big questions: What is your best way of working? What are the styles of your team members, and how do you relate to them today? How can you build bridges and knock down barriers to working more effectively? A first step in answering these questions is to understand the four different styles described below:

Ethan's company provides high-tech instruments that help manufacturers find defects in their products. He leads a team of three managers, each of whom directs a team of 5 to 10 people responsible for different phases of implementing the products in customers' businesses. Ethan's management style is collaborative, and he leads a meeting three times a week to discuss external and internal issues and solutions. If someone is having difficulty with a customer, he often joins the discussion, because he's a great listener and resolves conflicts with win-win proposals.

Nichole is the manager responsible for getting the instruments installed and working at customer sites. Her team, many of whom work on-site with customers, shares detailed plans and schedules daily. Nichole's natural style is quietly detail oriented: she prizes her team's diligence when it comes to delivering solutions on time, on schedule, and on budget.

Chloe heads a new team that creates video and interactive training for customers to take advantage of the company's newest technology. Her greatest pleasure is working with the company's marketing department and creative professionals to make training that is never boring but always relevant. Chloe is a big-picture thinker; lately she's partnered with a person in marketing to adapt training video to social media, reaching new potential customers.

Rounding out the team is Josh, who leads a group of technical experts that customize the company's defect-tracking solutions for different needs. Josh also reports to a technical lead in the CTO's office, where he has created a system that takes customer needs and use cases to help improve the next generation of products.

These four managers bring different strengths and knowledge to a range of services that are useful to customers and to the company. They often work virtually, and their meetings are never status updates but instead focus on solving problems, creating opportunities, and keeping in close touch with each other and different parts of the company. Their different styles are not impediments to working well; in fact, they're part of working well together.

When you understand your own work style and the styles of each member of your team, you draw a road map to success. Like us, you can learn to do work that is broader and better than individual team members could do by themselves.

What Is a Workplace Style?

Think of your workplace style as the sum of your temperament, tastes, cultural beliefs, skills, habits, and all the choices you make through a day that guide your behavior. That's a lot to think about, but even a brief consideration of *why* you do *what* you do shows patterns that coalesce into a recognizable picture.

Most people are familiar with some of the temperament and personality assessments used to help them understand themselves and/or others. Some popular examples (and their variations) are the Myers-Briggs Type Indicator, Gallup's CliftonStrengths, DiSC, the Predictive Index, and the Five-Factor Model. They are popular because they are easy-to-understand templates that apply to different settings. How effective they are in real-world settings depends on the skill with which their insights are applied.

Deloitte created a diagnostic tool called Business Chemistry® that informs our work. The descriptions of the people above are based on its model. We won't offer a comprehensive description of it here (the creators do that in their book, *Business Chemistry*[1]). Instead, we'll use its model to talk about the interaction of *relationships* and *well-being* at work—how and why you should seek to maximize the quality of both.

Business Chemistry organizes the broad range of individual temperaments into easily understood types:

> *Pioneers* value possibilities and spark energy and imagination. Pioneers are outgoing, spontaneous, and adaptable. They are enthusiastic risk takers and creative thinkers, great at generating ideas and prize variety. In the example above, Chloe is a Pioneer.
>
> *Guardians* value stability and bring order and discipline to work. Guardians are practical, detail oriented, and typically reserved. They are deliberate decision makers, persistent and loyal. Teams rely on them to keep processes on track. Nichole is a Guardian.
>
> *Drivers* thrive on challenge and generate momentum. They are technical, quantitative, and logical, and they can be quite direct in their approach to people and problems. Drivers want to know the reason for everything. They can make quick decisions, and they love winning. Josh is a Driver.
>
> *Integrators* prize connection and draw teams together. Integrators use their empathy and diplomatic skills to build relationships among a group. They are attuned to nuance, living in a world of words, feelings, relationships, and subtle connections. Trust and respect—both giving and receiving—are highly important to them. Ethan is an Integrator.

Every good model of temperament notes that nobody is 100 percent one type. For example, Jen is primarily an Integrator who is skilled at building relationships and understanding other people. This is invaluable because she has to consider the vast diversity of 100,000 Deloitte employees in the United States, establishing alliances and gaining buy-in to new practices across many cultures. Her secondary type is the Pioneer, which suits her role as one of the first chief well-being officers in the world. She is energized by the challenge of inventing a new role and new ways to promote well-being.

Anh is an example of how one's understanding of type might evolve. She would describe her style earlier in her career as a Driver-Guardian, managing technology initiatives and client service in a heavily quantitative field. But over time she realized she's more naturally a Pioneer (which is why she switched from client service to research) and balances her Driver tendencies with strong Integrator leanings (leading both in-person and remote teams). "People were always important to me personally," she says, "But over time I realized that those strong work relationships were also the key to being most effective in my job."

The authors of *Business Chemistry* note that personality and work-style assessments are ubiquitous, and we'd bet that readers of this book already have a pretty good idea of their own temperaments.[2] The next question is, how does your type translate into your daily behavior? How can you use that knowledge to improve personal and team performance in the current workplace we've described—fast-changing, interdependent, requiring all sorts of talents and temperaments to stay ahead?

Imagine a company that creates, manufactures, and sells a consumer product—let's say toys. The business relies on a steady stream of new creations as well as a whole ecosystem to bring ideas from brainstorming to consumer purchase. The company needs Integrators to help teams work together creatively, and to facilitate communication across different departments and help everyone do their best work. It needs Guardians who manage complex project demands of scheduling, purchasing, manufacturing, and delivering products, coordinating the work of many different teams, often in different countries. Drivers might question the status quo of all kinds of processes, from prototyping (perhaps using 3D printing or computer modeling) to manufacturing. And

Pioneers might be the stars of the creative teams, creating break-through ideas that result in next year's must-have toy.

Each business, department, and team needs some of these qualities in different degrees. A tax preparation department can use a lot of Guardians and Drivers. A marketing department, which is a natural place for Pioneers and Integrators, also needs people who are at least somewhere on the Guardian scale, from proofreaders to data analysts, to ensure quality. Even the most buttoned-down tax department can use the skills of an Integrator to help promote well-being, supportive relationships, and clear communication.

The Temperament Spectrum

Temperament explains only part of performance. It's a look into why people are energized by some tasks and struggle with others. Because nobody is 100 percent one type, their work styles are most accurately viewed as falling on a series of behavioral spectrums.

For example, one familiar spectrum along which we consider people's work style is introversion and extroversion. Although popular clichés abound—introverts are nerds, and extroverts are glad-handing sales executives—research tells us that the truth is more subtle. People live their lives between the extremes, being somewhat introverted or somewhat extroverted.[3] A good way to look at the difference between them is that introverts are energized by working independently or in small groups, and extroverts are energized by working with other people or in busy, activity-filled places.

Understanding your tendencies and preferences helps you design a work life in which you are using your talents and skills at their best. That is only a beginning, however. The "practical magic" of understanding others' types, and how to work with them best, is the gateway to proficiency in today's interdependent work world. When you understand others' best ways of working, you can leave the notion that there is one "best way" of working in every situation. And because so much changes so fast in our work today, understanding how people tick and how to bridge the differences among them is a big part of managing change.

The spectrum from introversion to extroversion is just one axis of temperament; many more are relevant when considering your workplace style. They manifest as preferences for certain behaviors or points of view. For example, point to a place on the following scale that you believe corresponds to your temperament:

Conciliatory	←――――――→	Dominating
Cooperative	←――――――→	Competitive
Cautious	←――――――→	Risk taking
Goal oriented	←――――――→	Relationship oriented
Prefers individual work	←――――→	Prefers teamwork
Structured	←―――――→	Adaptable
Detail oriented	←―――――→	Big-picture oriented
Quantitative	←――――――→	Qualitative

When you read these examples, did you find yourself judging whether one behavior was "better" or "worse"? Words become freighted with meaning by our personal preferences, our experiences, and our values. One person's "Dominating" means bold leadership, while another person's "Dominating" means bossy. To one person, "Conciliatory" means "finding common ground," and to another, it means "giving in." Your reaction is a clue to your preferences.

If you want to take this exercise one step further, share it with a trusted colleague and ask, "Do you agree that's where I fall on the scale? How about you?" Talk about how you might bridge the gaps in how you communicate with specific people. For example, do you tend to focus on the big picture and get bored when others focus on details? Both are important perspectives, but their value is realized only when people acknowledge their mutual value. Discussions about differences offer surprising insights in how you perceive both yourself and others.

Culture and Relationships

Organizational cultures also identify with places along spectrums of values. Sometimes entire cultures are built around an ethos of winning. Other companies, like Patagonia, are famous for a culture that puts people and planet first.[4] Some center their culture on innovation (Netflix), delighting customers (Disney), or employee engagement and fun (Zappos). All these cultures can produce success in business terms, but organizations must also adapt to changing times, which means the ways in which they act on their values might change. Cultures that thrive through change preserve their values even as they change their methods, business models, technology, and other factors.

Culture and Temperament

When people act out of shared values, their differences in temperament and skills are a strength. Company culture is the real-world sum of the hundreds of ways in which values are lived among people at work (and their customers).

Let's imagine two people in a company that prides itself on its "winning" culture. Sam is an introvert who likes to work alone, preparing pricing models for the sales department. He rocks the spreadsheets and creates clear, compelling charts. His boss, Carol, is a prototypical sales manager, outgoing and voluble, always keeping an eye on the quarterly numbers. Though their temperaments differ, they have an effective partnership because Sam supplies Carol with the data she needs to present a great solution to potential customers. Both Sam and Carol are engaged in "winning" according to their own individual styles. They express the same culture in different ways.

Looking deeper, we find that Sam and Carol share more than the company's culture of winning—it's their *relationship* that makes them effective. They trust each other on many levels: Carol knows that she can ask Sam for last-minute changes to a presentation and he'll get it done, quickly and accurately. Sam knows Carol respects his work and trusts him without insisting he act like her. Even though her ebullient persona is the opposite of his quiet, shy demeanor, Carol never tells Sam to lighten up or change himself. Though she sometimes thinks Sam could benefit from sitting through a high-stakes sales call, she understands that he doesn't communicate comfortably with strangers. She also knows his work will improve if he can anticipate the tough questions that come in such sales calls. And so Carol and Sam have come up with a mutually beneficial solution: she privately asks him to explain and defend his pricing strategies as if she were the customer, asking the questions the customer would ask and recognizing Sam for the insights he teaches her.

This relationship between introvert and extrovert is meaningful to both; it's grounded in trust and confidence in each other's different talents, mutually respectful of their differences and focused on common goals. Both have learned to put their own strengths into building that meaningful relationship—and building those relationships is part of the company's culture of winning. Yes, the culture measures winning in terms of sales numbers, beating the competition, coming out on top in business terms. And it also says winning needs strong relationships to get the best out of everyone.

The "winning" culture of Sam and Carol's organization enables both introverts and extroverts to work toward a common goal even as their temperaments and work styles are polar opposites. Their meaningful, positive, and mutually trusting relationship derives from the shared value of winning and the shared value of respect. As a result, the winning culture is not a zero-sum game of one of them winning and one losing in every interaction, but a culture of teamwork that means winning together.

Large organizations have subcultures as well. A pharmaceutical company will have some people focused on preventing disease and others focused on curing disease, which call for different perspectives.[5] Employees of a state university can unite around the goal of excellent, affordable education—and you'll find a wide range of subcultures there, from the college of dentistry to the bursar's office to the athletics department to the law school.

The culture of a global organization doesn't ask employees in Spain, Japan, or India to set aside all the traditions and cultural markers of their homelands. Rather, it says, "Express these shared values in the ways that are comfortable and appropriate for yourself and your colleagues."

It's the *relationships*—how interactions play out between employees—that show the true nature of an organization's culture. In the language of Deloitte's Business Chemistry, Guardian Sam and Pioneer Carol have built a relationship in which they each get what they need and give their best to benefit the common mission. They don't have to change who they are; they do have to honor the differences between them.

Well-Being and Relationships

We are focused on bringing "well-being" into the flow of work, and meaningful "relationships" are foundational to well-being in the workplace. To see how they work together, we first have to define just what we mean by those two terms that are often misunderstood.

When we speak to an audience, we're often asked about "well-ness," but the scope of well-being is more expansive than the famil-iar practices of wellness. Wellness at work is the idea that employers should promote physical and mental health and has led to many worthy programs from smoking cessation to weight management to employee referral programs for mental health. Well-being is a holistic approach—it includes physical, mental, financial well-being and a sense of purpose. It means supporting people with the flexibility they need to focus on what matters most to them. It's about the whole self and recognizing that well-being is unique to each individual (and their families), and that those unique needs can change throughout a person's life journey. In fact, social psychologists avoid the term "happiness" and use a more precise term, "subjective well-being," to indicate that everyone experiences pleasure, satisfaction, contentment, and other elevated moods at particular times and intensities and in their individual ways.[6] Well-being appears to be the ultimate subjective experience.

Well-being asks us to consider how workplace practices can support the whole person. For example, we've heard about "work-life balance" for decades, but that language implies that work and life have equal weight throughout a career. At different times, work and life can't be equal. Sometimes a work challenge is so invigo-rating, and offers such great reward, that it will take precedence over outside interests. At other times, such as a big life event like becoming a parent or surviving an illness, life outside of work is the priority. As work-life balance has become embedded in our business structures, it's often reliant on approval and support from one's supervisors, or on formal programs like six weeks of paren-tal leave (and no more) that ultimately assert the primacy of work.

Well-being's holistic view is more suited to the concept of work-life integration, which we're happy to say has gained traction over the last decade. Work-life integration as it's practiced pro-motes self-control, self-advocacy, and self-design of one's career. It engages individual employees by asking them to help design how work should best fit into their lives, while at the same time keeping the business goals in mind.

We saw a lot of action around work-life integration during the COVID-19 pandemic. People stepped up to learn new skills of teleworking, videoconferencing, and accomplishing work despite their disrupted schedules. And the companies that truly walked the talk of well-being accommodated those people with choices in technology, flexible work hours, and reallocated assignments. As an improvisation, it wasn't always perfect (in some places, parents, and especially mothers, were asked to do double duty, not letting up on their workload but still caring for children when schools closed), but it was an opportunity for the true believers to say yes, we can change how we work for the sake of someone's well-being.

Well-being goes beyond physical and mental health, beyond financial needs and the gratification of working toward a mission. It embraces the fact that people crave meaning in their lives and that there are many ways to achieve a sense of meaning. For some people it's great accomplishment or wealth or prestige. For others it means spiritual growth or social service, and their job's meaning is that it makes those things possible. Some find meaning because their work supports their families or communities. Others might devote themselves to a passion entirely unrelated to work, such as pursuing a musical or artistic career while supporting themselves with gig work.

Becoming Deloitte's chief well-being officer was part of Jen's well-being journey. She says: "In a former role, I was doing a poor job of setting boundaries. I was go, go, go—working most of my awake hours, and sleeping with my phone next to me. Because I was exercising for one hour every day, I thought I was taking care of myself. But, in fact, I ended up suffering from burnout to the point that I couldn't get out of bed. My mentor saw I was not well and really pressed me about my mental and physical health. She also encouraged me to take a professional step back, heal, and figure out what I wanted to do next. After some recovery time, I went to her and told her I needed to leave Deloitte so that I could do something in the well-being space. She instead encouraged me to propose a role like the one I have now, and her argument was that if I needed to learn how to prioritize my well-being, then others did too. Because Deloitte places such a high value on its people, this role came to fruition. Over the last almost five years, the role has evolved, and so have I, but well-being is always at the forefront."

Integrating Well-Being into the Workplace

Whereas wellness programs are typically thought of as outside the daily routine of work, well-being means integrating positive habits and behaviors into the routine. When employees feel the connection between personal well-being and good organizational outcomes, they bypass the expectation that well-being practices are a bolt-on to the workday. They lose self-consciousness about practicing good physical, emotional, mental, and financial habits even as they do their jobs.

One factor in well-being is a feeling of autonomy—that you have a degree of power over your work—and teams can plan this into their workweek. To empower individuals, teams can plan "no-meeting Wednesdays" for uninterrupted work time prioritized by each person. Jen's team has experimented with "Learning Fridays" in which the 2 p.m. to 4 p.m. period every Friday is reserved for learning or sharpening skills. Instead of trying to cram learning into evenings or weekends, every team member knows that paid time is dedicated to growth. Well-being activities thus become planned directly into work, and this permission and predictability elevates well-being to the status it merits. (We'll say more about specific well-being practices for teams and individuals in Chapters 5, 6, and 7.)

Knowing and acting on your work style and the style of others is a particularly effective way to bring well-being into work. In the example of Sam and Carol above, each understands the other's styles and strengths and respects the differences. Sam and Carol can collaborate with integrity because they trust each other. There's no need for image management or power games, and that means less stress, more productivity, and a greater sense of belonging for each. Sam and Carol don't have to go to the gym to work off stress based on office politics (although they're free to go to the gym for the right reasons!). Their workplace culture, expressed in a hundred different interactions, bolsters well-being.

Organizations that restructure work to promote well-being help employees not only feel and perform their best, both individually and in teams. In Deloitte's 2020 survey of global human capital trends, respondents said that their well-being strategy improved the workforce experience, reputation in the market, customer experience, financial outcomes, innovation, and adaptability. They ranked well-being the most important trend even before the COVID-19 pandemic made well-being an urgent concern.[7] In the spring of 2020, practices like flexible schedules, telecommuting, reallocation of tasks, and reimbursement for well-being expenses like ergonomic office equipment suddenly became more than an office-based benefit; they were the way employees and companies kept going.

There's a psychological payoff to this as well, because as well-being becomes part of daily work, it promotes a shared sense of caring about the whole person. People feel better stating their needs, and there's less pressure to "look busy." In Deloitte's 2018 human capital trends survey, 43 percent of respondents said well-being reinforces their organization's mission and vision, and 63 percent said it improves employee retention.[8]

Beware Work-Style Myths

Our understanding of work style in ourselves and others can be distorted by myths about people at work. Even when we learn about factors like temperament, personality, and values, we still work in an environment filled with obvious and subtle ideas about the right and wrong ways to work. That these ideas are myths hardly diminishes their power because they are the mental landscape for all the interactions of the day.

Consider friendships at work. On one end of the spectrum, there's the belief that work is no place for friendships. "It's just business; nothing personal." People with this belief might use it as an excuse to disrespect colleagues, or take unfair advantage, or just detach from friendly interactions. They might be a corporate shark, or they just might be really shy. They might simply believe that friendship adds nothing practical to work. One's temperament is less relevant than one's motivations and behavior.

On the other end of the friendship spectrum, there's the pretense that you have to develop friendly relationships with everyone in order to be successful, and that even the team member whom you find obnoxious should somehow be your good buddy. People who fear conflict, and cover disagreement by pretending it doesn't exist, preserve the myth of friendship when it's not the reality.

Discarding the myths, we come to the healthy realization that people form friendships at work for the same reasons they happen outside of work: mutual trust, enjoyment of company, shared ideas and values, an interest in the whole person, and caring. It's insincere to pretend to like everyone equally (not to mention exhausting); yet it's isolating to set friendships aside entirely.

Instead, a balanced view sees friendships at work as something good that is part of well-being for individuals and teams. Friendships increase the quality of life at work.

Jen is often asked, "Should work be fun?" The answer is an emphatic *yes!*, but the fact that the question is even asked is revealing. People think fun is not serious, and work has to be endlessly serious, and therefore there's no place for fun at work. They think, "I won't be taken seriously (and thus granted power, responsibility, prestige, promotions) if clients/customers/employees see me enjoying myself."

There are many reasons this is wrong. Here are just a few:

- Fun can help increase engagement.
- Enjoying work, experiencing pleasure both in the work itself and in the relationships, is energizing.
- Fun helps people bond and relieves stress.
- Creation is fun, and fun can be highly creative.
- Humor is an effective way to communicate and a relationship builder.
- When you don't take yourself too seriously, you give permission for others to lighten up as well. It cuts through all the layers of status and power people use to distance themselves from others.
- Different people have fun in different ways; sharing them is showing parts of yourself others might not know, which builds trust. (Provided your idea of "fun" isn't embarrassing or offensive to others.)

During the first few weeks of the COVID-19 pandemic, we observed that our teleconferences were formal. People who had not worked remotely before were stressed by the new routine. But soon we were struck by the ingenious ways people found to socialize at a distance. There were teleconference happy hours. A group took a virtual tour of an animal sanctuary together. Another group, noticing that members were watching more video at home, shared suggestions on the topic of "Best movies you've never seen." Each week a different member would list a classic or forgotten movie, and then members would watch and the following week close their work meeting with a 10-minute discussion of the hidden treasure they'd found. They maintained their personal connections by having a bit of fun together.

Here are a few other myths about people's work styles or workplace that we've collected.

Longer Work Hours Means Greater Productivity

We cited this myth in Chapter 1. Despite studies that show everyone has a limit of productive hours in a day or a week, it persists. Burnout is not a badge of honor.

Money Is the Only Motivator

This myth arises from the fact that financial reward is the easiest motivator to measure. It's powered up by a culture that celebrates wealth as the measure of someone's worth. It's also simpleminded; studies show that motivation and engagement at work are the result of many factors, including feelings like being appreciated and doing meaningful work, which vary from person to person.[9] Motivation is also localized in the sense that employee loyalty is more a factor of how people feel about their immediate managers and their teams. Numerous psychology studies show that intrinsic motivators (such as a sense of purpose, meaning, loyalty) are more powerful than extrinsic motivators, such as money.

Most People Don't Really Want to Work Hard

Few people are naturally lazy, but lots of people—maybe most of the employees we call "disengaged"—don't want to put energy into a job they don't believe in. The solution for that isn't to call them lazy but to discover why they don't believe in the job, because a mediocre workplace has endless ways to kill motivation and energy. It could be a bad boss. It could be that the job's importance to the organization's success isn't clear. It could be that the value of the work is unacknowledged. It could be the deadening weight of bureaucracy or frustration because "my work will never see the light of day." Maybe some people are just in the wrong job, applying their weak skills instead of their greatest strengths. Perhaps some people are simply never recognized for working hard. Or maybe they are not challenged enough and are bored. There are a thousand ways to de-energize people, and the traditional organization is very good at that.

You don't need to go further than remembering a time you were really energized by a project. Remember that feeling of "flow" when you poured energy effortlessly into the work. Now remember a time when you had to drag yourself through a project you didn't care about (we've all had them). Note the differences between the two projects, and you'll see that what we call laziness is more a product of the situation than an innate quality.

Knock down barriers to caring, and the energy will follow.

Different Work Styles Are Required for Relationships, Making Things Happen, Leading and Following

This is a misconception people bring to the assessments we discussed earlier. People love to typecast others. Remember that everyone is a mix of characteristics, however, and different styles express strengths in different ways. It's true that Integrators tend to be good at forming relationships, and that reflects both their natural empathy and the ease with which they communicate, but it's also true that Pioneers tend to be good at inspiring others to be their best, which is a priceless kind of relationship. Drivers make great coaches with their detachment and analytical powers, and their students are devoted to them because of that relationship. And Guardians are loyal to a fault, generating a kind of trustworthiness that's the foundation of healthy relationships.

Work Is a Zero-Sum Game

This is another misconception based on traditional power hierarchies. It's the product of a scarcity mindset. The rules of human nature and capitalism alike debunk this myth, because at their best, both are about people coming together to grow the total rewards, both material and psychological, available to all.

This myth is the basis for so much wasted effort, self-censorship, and mediocre business results that it brings us to the next chapter—how to make your relationships at work, work for all.

KEY POINTS

- A work style is the sum of temperament, beliefs, skills, habits, and all the choices you make through a day that guide your behavior.
- Individual and group behaviors fall somewhere on a spectrum between extremes.
- Strong relationships enable people to work well together, not despite their differences, but because they leverage their different strengths.
- Well-being goes beyond wellness, and honoring differences is one way to design well-being directly into work.

CHAPTER 5

TEAM VALUES AND BEHAVIOR

Organizations' results depend almost entirely on teams
. . . humans have accomplished almost everything
we've ever accomplished in our history in groups.

—Thomas Malone, founder of the MIT Center for Collective
Intelligence, MIT Sloan School of Management

We saw in Chapter 2 how important relationships are to well-being, and also that relationships are the foundation of effective work in organizations. Yet despite all evidence to the contrary, old habits and attitudes about work keep pushing us to devalue relationships as we devalue our health. As Jen's story of approaching burnout testified, there's a tidal pull from personal habits and business cultures that keeps putting business results before well-being or healthy relationships.

That's an obsolete viewpoint. Well-being and healthy relationships are foundational to business results, not an impediment to them. In 2020, *Deloitte's Global Human Capital Trends* report found that, for the first time, well-being was a top concern of executives. They perceive that both well-being and strong relationships are essential to the interdependent, team-based workplace.[1]

Another top concern the report found was the importance of employees feeling a sense of belonging at the organization. It said, "Workers should feel *comfortable* at work, including being treated fairly and respected by their colleagues. They should feel *connected* to the people they work with and the teams they are part of. And they should feel that they *contribute* to meaningful work outcomes—understanding how their unique strengths are helping their teams and organizations achieve common goals."[2]

Comfort, connection, and contribution drive belonging. When you look a little deeper, you recognize that all three are the result of healthy relationships with one's team members.

Well-being and healthy relationships are defining characteristics of strong, long-lasting teams, and yet they are too often thrown into that bucket of qualities we think of as nice-to-haves. The typical company culture puts qualities like excellence, innovation, knowledge, financial performance, or industry leadership at the top, while losing sight of the fact that these are the result of strong and healthy people working well together. When a company relegates well-being and healthy relationships to its second tier of values, it's like a sports team of talented players who don't stay healthy and don't learn to work together. Perhaps the team will perform well for a while, but it won't reach its full potential or remain on top for long.

The Values Quadrant

We picture the dynamics of a workplace according to how much it values well-being and strong relationships. You can see how these influence workplace culture by laying them over a simple four-quadrant grid, with the *x*-axis representing the degree to which a culture values individual well-being, and the *y*-axis representing the degree to which it values relationships among employees, as shown in Figures 5.1 and 5.2.

VALUES RELATIONSHIP

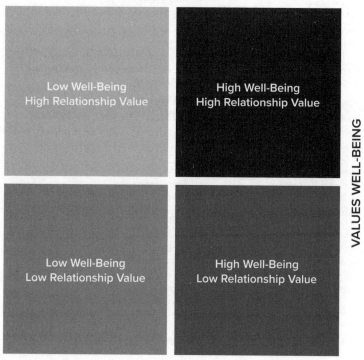

FIGURE 5.1 Each quadrant represents a different workplace culture.

The interplay between these values—strong and weak on each axis—creates quadrants that represent workplace cultures familiar in organizational life. We'll describe each below, counterclockwise from top left. Each description includes the characteristics of the quadrant, its results for people and the organization, ways to address the situation, and (to make it memorable) a mascot and nickname representing the quadrant.

VALUES RELATIONSHIP

SCHOOL OF SHARKS	TRUSTED TEAMS
Relationships focused entirely on getting business results. Well-being efforts either hidden or window dressing.	Well-being brought into the flow of work, focusing on trust, managing diverse temperaments, awareness, and group reliance habits.
RESULT: **Burnout** • High turnover • Low morale • High healthcare costs	RESULT: **Sustainable Results** • Team and individual well-being • Resilience • Innovation, risk taking
MASCOT: **Shark**	MASCOT: **Dolphin**
TO DO: Realign teamwork, give permission for well-being. Practice Radical Candor.	TO DO: Sustain with cultural acts of bonding, cooperation, and individual wellness practices.

DOOM LOOP	LONE LEOPARDS
Unhealthy and dysfunctional, producing neither good business results nor healthy people.	Individual well-being but no shared vision of how relationships produce business results. Loner mentality.
RESULT: **Business Failure** • Apathy • Cynicism • Disengagement • Low-performance culture	RESULT: **Lost Opportunity** • Low innovation, risk taking • Low organizational resilience • Uneven engagement
MASCOT: **Opossum**	MASCOT: **Leopard** (solitary hunter)
TO DO: Change culture, change methods . . . before it's too late.	TO DO: Connect individual wellness to business results (including compensation, performance assessment). Teach teamwork.

VALUES WELL-BEING

FIGURE 5.2 Characteristics of workplace cultures.

As you read the descriptions, ask yourself, "Which of these cultures is most like my team, my division, and my company?"

1. The School of Sharks

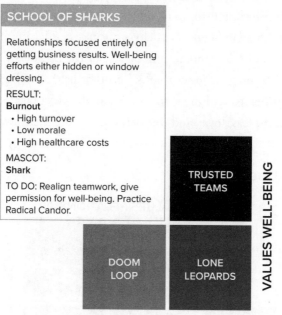

FIGURE 5.3 The School of Sharks: When relationships matter and well-being does not.

In the School of Sharks, shown in Figure 5.3, relationships matter, but well-being is unimportant. This workplace is characterized by focusing relationships entirely on their utility for getting business results, regardless of their genuine qualities. It's the height of workism: people work crazy hours and are expected to suck it up and not complain. Relationships are transactional—with others on the team, with people in the wider organization, and even with customers. Relationships are valued for their utility: acquiring money, success, or prestige. The School of Sharks is characterized by zero-sum thinking and a scarcity mindset; people react to limits on promotions and bonus money by grabbing the most they can for themselves.

This is a stereotypical version of a hard-driving workplace, where winners win and anyone who falters is lunch. The mascot of this workplace is the shark, always cruising for its next meal, with a few pilot fish clinging onto its sides hoping to pick up the leftovers.

The School of Sharks can deliver business results, but its human cost is burnout, low morale among all but the biggest sharks, high turnover among the lesser sharks (or other fish), and high cost of health. When the culture is transactional, the most talented people are often the least loyal, and competitors can lure them away.

2. The Doom Loop

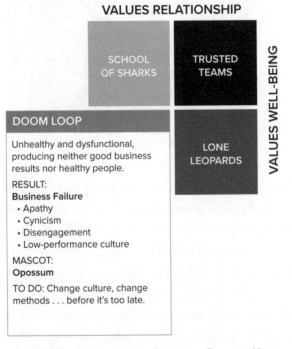

FIGURE 5.4 The Doom Loop: Business suffers as neither relationships nor well-being is valued.

If you've ever been in a workplace where neither relationships nor well-being matters, you probably shudder at the memory of participating in the Doom Loop, which is depicted in Figure 5.4. People might work very hard, disregarding their well-being, or just do the bare minimum, without a sense of purpose other than getting by. Business results on most metrics, from profits to employee engagement, are below average, and attempts to change such a culture are usually too little, too late. Apathy, cynicism, low performance, and a sense of drift characterize this workplace. This workplace has inspired decades of mordant humor in the strip *Dilbert*.

The Doom Loop's mascot is the opossum, which is shy, and when threatened falls into a catatonic state ("playing possum").[3]

3. Lone Leopards

VALUES RELATIONSHIP

SCHOOL OF SHARKS	TRUSTED TEAMS
DOOM LOOP	**LONE LEOPARDS**

VALUES WELL-BEING

LONE LEOPARDS

Individual well-being but no shared vision of how relationships produce business results. Loner mentality.

RESULT:
Lost Opportunity
• Low innovation, risk taking
• Low organizational resilience
• Uneven engagement

MASCOT:
Leopard (solitary hunter)

TO DO: Connect individual wellness to business results (including compensation, performance assessment). Teach teamwork.

FIGURE 5.5 Lone Leopards: Lack of teamwork produces uneven business results.

The Lone Leopard culture, shown in Figure 5.5, values individual well-being but not strong human relationships. That might be due to a culture of rugged individualism, or in some organizations, it might be due to the nature of the work itself (drivers in ride-hailing services, for example). For people who truly want to work alone, this isn't a bad place, but for most businesses it represents lost opportunity. Innovation and risk taking work best when trusted bonds exist among team members, so the team is weakened in this scenario. Organizational resilience is lower. With less understanding of contrasting work styles, individuals struggle to create win-win solutions. And while individuals might look out after themselves, they miss out on a well-being bonus: the feeling of meaning that comes from nurturing teamwork and genuine goodwill for others.

The leopard, which is strong and capable but lives most of its life alone, is our mascot for this workplace.

4. Trusted Teams

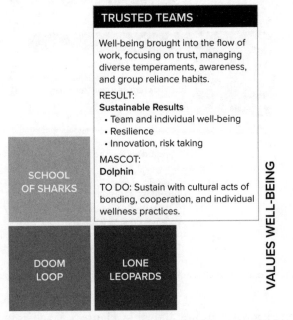

FIGURE 5.6 Trusted Teams: Positive relationships and well-being produce sustainable results.

A workplace that values both strong relationships and individual well-being is our ideal and is shown in Figure 5.6. We call this workplace Trusted Teams because individuals benefit when they look out for each other as well as themselves. This means much more than people being nice to one another. It means diverse types work together without forcing conformity. People give respect to and receive respect from peers and others at all levels of organizational authority. Training includes learning individual skills and also group dynamics. Trusted Teams benefit from an abundance mindset—the sense that work and life are full when they feed and restore each other. Organizational resilience grows from uniting around a common mission and purpose. Trusted teams are like the Blue Zones of living, where material, emotional, intellectual, and social needs are in balance.

Our mascot for Trusted Teams is the dolphin. Dolphins are intensely social creatures that communicate constantly, look out for each other, and are also capable on their own. And when they're not working—raising young or hunting—dolphins love to play!

Where Is Your Team?

Does one of these scenarios describe your team best? Remember that teams, like people, rarely exist at one extreme or the other. Your team might have a couple of sharks and a few dolphins (who keep sharks at a distance). Or someone working in a Doom Loop situation might be checked out emotionally but taking care of her own well-being for a time, waiting it out until a better opportunity arises. Consider who you are (or want to be) and who others are in your immediate work circle. Are you surrounded by people with the same values, and could you all name what they are? While we would ideally work in Trusted Teams, we know that some cultures and people consciously choose another way of being together.

Try this informal exercise: Decide which scenario best describes your team and write the reasons for your decision. If a definitive answer doesn't spring to mind, you might point to a place on the chart where you'd put your team, as demonstrated in Figure 5.7.

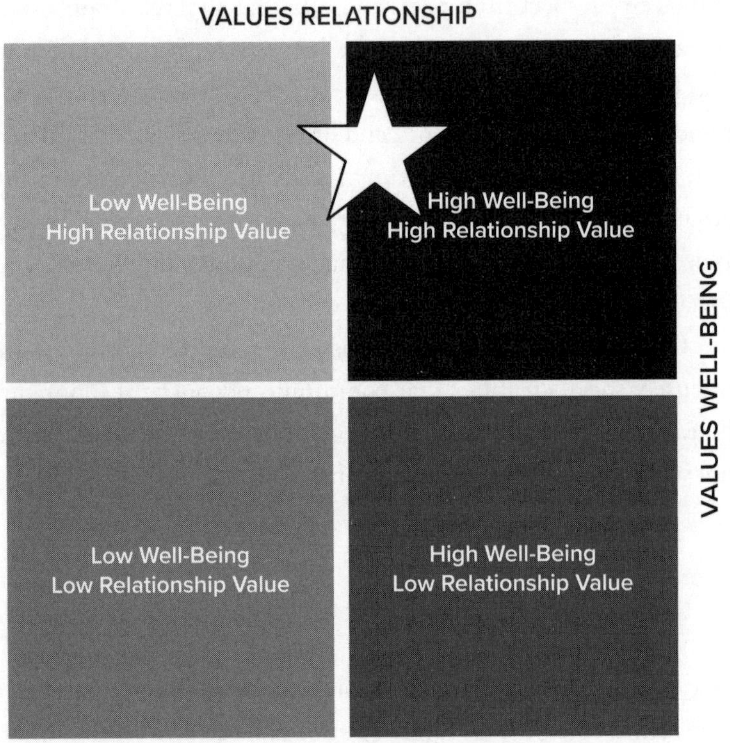

VALUES RELATIONSHIP

Low Well-Being High Relationship Value	High Well-Being High Relationship Value
Low Well-Being Low Relationship Value	High Well-Being Low Relationship Value

VALUES WELL-BEING

FIGURE 5.7 In which quadrant does your organization fit?

This team values relationships more intensely than it values well-being. The members of the team strive to work together well, and people feel that they belong, but individual well-being is a nice-to-have quality. This is typical for a high-performance culture where people are reluctant to put their needs before the needs of the group, even when it's important to them. "Friendships are fine, but business comes first" might be their motto.

So where's your team? You might think of your immediate group led by a single manager, or a department where you work. Read on and come back to this concept of where you are on the grid, because as you consider the interplay of relationships and well-being, you might want to revise your view.

Remember, you're thinking about two axes here: how much your group values relationships and how much it values well-being. You can use a major-minor concept that temperament assessments like Business Chemistry use. For example, your team might feel like it's mostly Lone Leopards, focused on individual well-being, but sometimes you focus on building stronger relationships among team members (like people do in team-building exercises at the beginning of a new project or a new team configuration). In that case, you'd inch into Trusted Teams territory.

It helps to consider your immediate team members first. As we noted in Chapter 4, teams are collections of individual temperaments, and an effective team might include introverts and extroverts, Guardians and Integrators, Pioneers and Drivers. All can value relationships or well-being differently; this exercise is asking you to consider what the team's culture is telling you.

Try writing the name of each team member and which quadrant he or she would naturally fall into. Again, feel free to use the same major-minor concept that temperament assessments like Business Chemistry does; e.g., "Cindy is a dolphin most of the time, and a shark in high-pressure situations. She values strong relationships at all times but can get into burnout mode when business results are on the line."

It's worthwhile to discuss where your team is on the quadrant among team members. Do you agree on where you are? Are you happy with that, or might there be ways to move toward a better state? The conversation doesn't have to provide a definitive answer but act as a jumping-off point for the ongoing discussion about making your team good for relationships and well-being.

The Power of Working in Teams

Matt Calcagno, a former colleague of Anh's, offers this description of the many ways a well-functioning team depends on genuine human connection:

> As a socially driven person, I inherently find much of my motivation and fulfillment when delivering with the help and company of a team. Macroscopically, working as a team, united by a common mission, makes it easier to find purpose each day. I'm not working just to create a product or publish an article, but also to help each of my team members accomplish goals that we had set together and independently. In the day-to-day, having a team to lean on for support and encouragement during tough professional and even personal challenges is invaluable. I love that each of my accomplishments isn't celebrated in silence because my successes are contributing to the overall progress of the team. Sure, independently we can all accomplish a lot, but together we complement each other's strengths and weaknesses and go farther faster while having more fun along the way. Without a team by my side to huddle together during deadline season or to laugh with while rolling pasta there would undoubtedly be less meaning in my day.

The Qualities of Trusted Teams

The types of relationships you have at work matter to your well-being. It's not just about everyone getting along okay and going out for drinks or coffee every now and then. People need a deeper sense that their coworkers value the talents they have, respect their opinions, and actually care about them as human beings.

Research has found that the answers to the following three questions give a good indicator of positive relationships. All three are components of Trusted Teams:

Is diversity of thought valued in my group? Is groupthink our habit—or do we actively seek different ways of solving a problem? Do we value different temperaments and approaches, which drive innovation?

Can I share my own perspectives? Can I express a creative idea, a different point of view, a personal experience that differs from others', or a contrary opinion without being ignored or shut down?

Do I feel those I work with care about my well-being? Where is your group on the grid's x-axis? You can care about your own well-being and not care about the well-being of others (that's the Lone Leopards' scenario), but when people genuinely care about each other's well-being, they work better as a team.

People who answer an emphatic *yes!* to these three questions feel like they belong, which is the opposite of alienation and detachment. When you feel you belong because of your unique set of skills and temperament, rather than in spite of them, you are in a group with the potential to perform well. People who feel they belong are psychological stakeholders in their shared success.

How's your group? Do you think everyone has the same sense of belonging? If not, there are bridges to be built and barriers to be broken down, and we'll talk about those in the next chapter. Before you move along to those steps, let's consider the reasons that valuing both strong relationships and individual well-being make teams perform at their highest potential.

First, valuing both relationships and well-being creates a sense of belonging. People who study diversity, equity, and inclusion

(DEI) have in recent years paid more attention to belonging. DEI has gone beyond the concept of hiring people of different races, genders, backgrounds, abilities, etc., into a company, which is diversity. It's gone beyond just equity and inclusion, which means diverse people have a seat at the table, a share of the power, authority, and rewards. Belonging means that diverse people know that the organization isn't "them and me" but "all of us" and that the organization means it. This feeling cannot come from slogans or the best intentions of the C-suite or the board of directors. It can only be realized at the level of teams—the people with whom you work every day.

What prevents a sense of belonging? Obviously if someone is rejected or scorned by a group, but typically it happens in subtler ways such as withholding approval or access to information. People will go a long way to feel they belong, and there is a downside to this need. The risk was well described by Brené Brown when she wrote, "Belonging is the innate human desire to be part of something larger than us. Because this yearning is so primal, we often try to acquire it by fitting in and by seeking approval, which are not only hollow substitutes for belonging, but often barriers to it."[4]

People crave authentic social interaction. Our ancient ancestors were born into small bands of hunting and gathering clans. In evolutionary terms, large groups like towns and cities—and companies and organizations—are relatively recent inventions. While we have learned to adapt to larger groups, we still have a limited capacity for close relationships (Oxford professor Robin Dunbar established the number at about 150).[5] When email and social media or all-hands company gatherings might mimic the experience of close contact with a larger number of people, they're the social equivalent of a sugar high—energizing but not really nutritious. Our strong relationships are with our teams.

Belonging has become a top organizational priority as people feel the polarization and instability of the world at large. An international study for the World Economic Forum found that frustration with the status quo and a growing sense of "us versus them" have led to a deepening distrust in societies at large.[6] Many people are turning to the smaller "tribes" of their workplace teams to satisfy that need to belong.[7]

The Gallup Organization found that "in meaningful moments, how others receive an employee's vulnerability is critical. It creates a loop: A great culture allows an employee to take vulnerable risks, and a positive response to vulnerability builds a great culture—and the opposite is just as true."[8]

Spectrums of Team Behavior

Just as your individual style is the sum of many individual factors (temperament, tastes, beliefs, etc.), your team's style is the sum of many interactive factors. Teams can be almost as complicated as individual people for the simple reason that they're made up of individuals. Team styles like the School of Sharks, Doom Loop, Lone Leopards, and Trusted Teams describe habitual ways of interacting, shared values, power structures, the team's demographic makeup, the experiences different people bring, the way the team uses technology, and other behaviors and attitudes.

Over time (often quite a short time), teams tend to settle along behavioral spectrums, similar to the way people do. Just as someone can say, "I'm more introverted than extroverted," teams can say, "We like to work in a structured, predictable way."

The far ends of each spectrum are defined by opposite values and behaviors. For example:

Power hierarchy	←——→	Democratic/shared power
Transparent	←——→	Opaque
Uniformity of thought	←——→	Diversity of thought
Solitary work	←——→	Interactive/group work
Recognition and gratitude	←——→	Anonymity
Structured	←——→	Adaptable
Conflict averse	←——→	Conflict embracing
Action oriented	←——→	Analysis oriented

Where is your team on each spectrum? Mark an estimate on each line and ask yourself, "Why is it there?" Why does your team tend toward solitary work? What does that say about the team's relationships and well-being? This could also be an activity that is done as a team activity, with each team member independently (to avoid groupthink) deciding where on each spectrum the team is and where the team member would like the team to be. The answers can be tallied anonymously or with attribution, and the team members can discuss where their perceptions and values align or where there are gaps.

The Business Case for Trusted Teams

We believe the strong work relationships and individual well-being that define Trusted Teams are a good in themselves, but it's appropriate to present evidence in business terms. Quantifiable results and logical connections prove that these are much more than nice-to-haves in today's organizations, and studies confirm that they create competitive advantage, save money, unite employees in purpose and mission, and facilitate the complex ways we work today.

Alison Beard of the *Harvard Business Review* summarized the benefits of strong relationships when she wrote: "Your social connections are a strong predictor of your cognitive functioning, resilience, and engagement. Studies show that people with supportive coworkers have more work life balance and are less stressed. Teams of friends perform better. Gallup has long highlighted that having a best friend at work makes you seven times more engaged, on average."[9]

The business benefits of Trusted Teams include belonging, engagement, knowledge sharing, trust, creativity and innovation, and positivity, with all their benefits:

> *Belonging.* A widespread feeling of belonging in the workplace can lead to a 56 percent increase in job performance, a 50 percent reduction in turnover risk, and a 75 percent decrease in employee sick days, according to a 2019 study by the workplace research firm BetterUp.[10] These numbers represent an enormous potential gain for companies with low degrees of belonging.
>
> *Engagement.* We've seen in studies like Gallup's engagement research that one of the strongest drivers of employee engagement is the degree of social connection among people at work.[11] Employee engagement has been the holy grail of HR and management practices since the concept was popularized in the bestselling book *First, Break All the Rules.* Increasing employee engagement positively affects business outcomes as diverse as productivity, retention, financial performance, and healthcare spending.[12] Because social connection drives engagement, it drives those results.
>
> *Knowledge sharing.* In an information economy, the observation that "knowledge is power" is an understatement. In the past, business cultures put a need-to-know cloak on a lot of information (facts) and knowledge (how to use facts to achieve goals). In a networked economy, however, information and

knowledge become more powerful as more users access it. Allowing for confidentiality or proprietary protections, sharing information widely in an organization is now standard practice. You want the product team to know what the marketing and financial teams are doing. The trouble with intense competition is that it encourages the withholding of information for personal advantage.

Trust. Among team members, trust is another quality that unites individual well-being and strong relationships. When team members trust each other to be respectful, truthful, and accountable for their words and actions, they devote mental and emotional energy to the tasks at hand, and don't waste it on self-protection. Trust manifests itself in little ways throughout the day. When you speak up without fear of sounding stupid or being ridiculed, that's trust. When you share information openly, that's trust. When you admit you're stumped by a problem or ask for help, that's trust.

Relationships built on trust facilitate problem solving. When team members agree to hash out conflicting ideas or opinions respectfully, they open themselves to the possibility that an out-of-the-box solution might be suggested. When team members invite the most withdrawn introvert to bring ideas to the table (or at least pass around a written idea), they increase the odds that everyone feels okay about throwing out ideas. As the saying goes, "Trust is hard won and easily lost," but it's a powerful bond among team members in stressful times and a shortcut to efficiency when the going is smooth.

Creativity and innovation. We know that innovation is critical to staying ahead in today's globalized economy. Finding new ways of solving problems, or creating products and services that delight people in new ways, has fueled much of the growth of modern business. Innovation occurs in many forms, including new products (smartphones, electric cars), services (ride-sharing and payment apps), and business models (search engines and other "free" services that monetize data, platforms that turn homeowners into hoteliers). Creativity and innovation thrive when the two factors we've just mentioned, knowledge sharing and trust, are present on teams and in an organization.

Positivity. Research shows that teams that care for each other, show interest in each other, take responsibility for each other, and support each other in big and small ways increase positive emotions at work. In turn, increased positivity on a team makes the team more productive in measurable ways. It increases creativity. It encourages loyalty and strengthens a team's resilience when facing setbacks or tackling difficult assignments. All of this shows up in business results. Researcher Kim Cameron of the University of Michigan wrote, "When organizations institute positive, virtuous practices they achieve significantly higher levels of organizational effectiveness—including financial performance, customer satisfaction, and productivity. . . . The more the virtuousness, the higher the performance in profitability, productivity, customer satisfaction, and employee engagement."[13]

The direct financial benefit of making well-being a workplace priority is a little less easy to quantify, because well-being is still evolving beyond traditional wellness. Direct comparisons to past health practices are complicated. Nevertheless, the indirect ROI of well-being is clear. Companies that make an authentic commitment to employee well-being gain bottom-line benefits through increased productivity and lower expenditures.[14]

For example, the American Psychological Association compared companies where senior leadership is involved and committed to well-being initiatives with companies where they are not.[15] The study found dramatic differences in employee attitudes, including:

- 91 percent of the supported group felt motivated to do their best versus 38 percent of the unsupported group.
- 91 percent of the supported group said they were satisfied with their job versus 30 percent of the unsupported.
- 91 percent of the supported group said they had a positive relationship with their managers versus 54 percent of the unsupported.
- 89 percent of the supported group would recommend the company as a good place to work versus 17 percent of the unsupported group.

The business consultancy Mercer states that health and well-being are the cornerstones of an energized workforce, and that energized employees are three times as likely as de-energized employees to be satisfied with the company (with no plans to leave). Relevant to today's demand that the workforce constantly increase its skills base, those employees are twice as likely to be excited about the prospect of reskilling.[16]

All these findings have financial consequences. For example, companies where employees don't feel motivated to do their best suffer from the opportunity cost of lost potential. Companies that employees recommend as a good place to work get better ratings on Glassdoor, one of the first places that talented candidates go to research companies. And job satisfaction lowers turnover with its attendant costs. (Sadly, less than 44 percent of survey respondents said the climate in their companies supports employee well-being. We have a long way to go on that score.)

Show Recognition and Gratitude

Our colleague Kelly Gaertner believes managers should find every opportunity, large and small, to show gratitude and recognition on their teams. She says:

> Recognition comes in all shapes and sizes; and while it's not a one-size-fits-all, it's important to recognize and show gratitude in the workplace. With the tumultuous year 2020 has brought, the need for this is ever increasing. Leverage formal recognition opportunities and couple them with informal ones that are meaningful and representative of you. Whether that's sending people a Starbucks gift card to treat them to their favorite drink just because, or a handwritten note after a big milestone—be genuine, mix it up, and practice this often. These small acknowledgments can go a long way and be more of a help than you'd ever imagine to those on your team.

The Human Case for Trusted Teams

Trusted Teams aren't replacements for smart technology, and on the frontiers of work, technology is not replacing humans but augmenting human performance. MIT professor Thomas Malone, author of *Superminds: The Surprising Power of People and Computers Thinking Together*, believes that our most human qualities are critical to the relationship of people and technology. He said in an interview in *Deloitte Review*:

> Just having a bunch of smart people isn't enough to make a smart group. Instead, we found three other characteristics that were significantly correlated with the group's collective intelligence. The first was the degree to which the

people in the group had what you might call social intelligence or social perceptiveness. . . . It turns out that when a group has a bunch of people who are good at this, the group is, on average, more collectively intelligent than when it doesn't. The second factor was how evenly people participated in the group's conversations. If you have one or two people in a group who dominate the conversation, then, on average, the group is less collectively intelligent than when people participate more evenly. And, finally, we found the group's collective intelligence was correlated with the proportion of women in the group. Having more women was correlated with more intelligent groups. It's important to understand, though, that the factor about female membership was mostly explained statistically by the factor about social intelligence.[17]

Full participation in group conversations and social intelligence increase collective intelligence. That corresponds with what we already know about the free exchange of ideas in Trusted Teams, where technology is not a threat but elevates everyone's capability because it enhances the most human qualities like social perceptiveness. In Anh's experience implementing new technologies, the groups whose members supported each other through change could better embrace the full advantages new technology gave.

Malone's concept of superminds argues that a knowledge-based economy puts a premium on collective intelligence. Raise a group's intelligence, and you raise the value it's capable of creating. In regard to technology increasing the exchange of information, knowledge, and other communication, he says, "Each company is a supermind. Realizing this gets us thinking about how we're 'in this together.'"[18]

Trusted Teams are tuned into the human factor at work, even if they don't contain a single Integrator and even when they are focused on outcomes first. They recognize that strong relationships and well-being accelerate performance. It's not just about the business case, however. The culture of Trusted Teams includes a commitment to nonbusiness factors like meaning, purpose, happiness, enjoyment, and friendship. We are aware that the case for these qualities is frequently relegated to the nice-to-have corner of a business discussion, to which we reply: Why would you spend so many hours of your life doing something that doesn't contribute to your happiness and that of your colleagues? Shouldn't work be fulfilling and fun as well as profitable? The powerful desire for security, power, prestige, and position (all related in the end to feelings of security) causes so many people we know to keep silent, and perhaps a bit embarrassed, about these beliefs.

ANH'S STORY—AN EVOLVING STYLE

My work style evolved from Driver-Guardian to Pioneer-Integrator/Driver as I became an advocate for my own Trusted Team. It was a natural evolution as I dug deeper into the ways in which personal relationships and organizational culture made teams more effective. I'll always focus on outcomes, but I've seen that outcomes are profoundly affected by the human element.

Take the example of bringing new technology online. You can have the best technology and do a flawless, customized implementation, but if the people aren't really embracing it, the value of that technology goes out the window. Often, people aren't afraid of the technology itself, but they're worried about their own performance with it. They're worried about their jobs—will they be unable to master the new technology or even be replaced by it?

> Previously as a dominant Driver, I didn't work naturally in the realm of people's feelings. I viewed tasks and goals as impartial targets to hit, which was motivating for me. Over time, I've learned that a lot of success or failure in technology (or new business models, or new methods, or innovation) depends on how well people deal with change and especially how teams deal with change. They have to value individual well-being because not everybody is going to handle change in the same way. And they have to value relationships because the team can't function at its optimal level unless everyone is dealing well with everyone else. A well-functioning team makes a technology implementation or adoption more likely to succeed, and the opposite is also true. Over time, I focused more on developing the skills of an Integrator, because helping people learn to work together was the critical factor in achieving outcomes, whether they are technology driven or not.

Emotion and Power

If social intelligence and emotional intelligence are so good for teams, why don't traditional company cultures put more emphasis on developing them? Part of the problem is the idea of "seriousness" we put into all things business (as if intelligence and relationships weren't serious!). Another challenge is that these qualities are hard to measure and thus hard to manipulate or manage. They can violate hierarchal traditions of power, in which the boss or senior team members assume authority. For example, what if the most junior member of the team is also the most socially or emotionally skilled? What role does he or she play in team dynamics?

The historical reason organizations turn their backs on emotion was shared with Jen by Dr. Dacher Keltner, founding director of the Greater Good Science Center and a professor of psychology at the University of California, Berkeley. He said that the idea of checking your emotions at the door "comes from old cultural biases against the emotions, which is probably gender bias from the time when work was more male [oriented]. You can trace back in a lot of different thinkers the idea that emotions are disruptive, they are dysfunctional, they are irrational."

Keltner, the author of *The Power of Emotion,* noted that "power really diminishes your empathy." Citing research from fellow academics like Suk Obendier and Keely Muscatell, he described interactions between low-power and high-power persons in an organization: the low-power person tends to mirror the high-power person, but the reverse is not true. In fact, a high-power person hearing a friend talk about a personal struggle has less active empathy networks in his brain than someone with a more equal power relationship to the friend.[19]

Behavior gives away the emotional changes power confers, says Keltner: "When you feel powerful, you become more impulsive. Even the basic parameters of emotion, like smiling and speaking more loudly. . . . the volume is turned up on all the impulsive emotions. You touch people too much because your approach-oriented emotions are more intense. When you feel low power, you feel anxious and worried and self-critical and ashamed. A life of less power is bad news for your body."[20]

Lack of power in a hierarchy is associated with stress and negative physical consequences. Chronic powerlessness is associated with elevated cortisol and increased inflammation in the body's immune system, which in turn is connected to heart disease, arthritis, diabetes, and other chronic illnesses.[21]

Sharing or not sharing power and showing or not showing emotion are powerful factors in the dynamics in each of the four team styles shown above. The School of Sharks values power as a way to get things done, but emotion is secondary—a traditional "business-first" view. In the Doom Loop, power is all but absent except for the remote bosses, and emotions might be negative or hidden. Lone Leopards flex their own kind of power by guarding their own interests, alert to what enables their well-being and emotional health but not very tuned into using emotional intelligence for the larger good. Trusted Teams use emotional intelligence as part of a sharing of power according to agreed norms such as expertise and decision-making responsibility.

You might be on any of the teams we've described. Whether you act like a shark, an opossum, a leopard, or a dolphin today, you also have the power to choose how much you value strong relationships and how much you value well-being. The next chapter lays out the many ways you can move toward your ideal.

KEY POINTS

- How much your team values strong relationships, and individual well-being, has a big impact on your ability to work effectively.
- Teams, like people, tend to express their style along a series of spectrums, rather than at the extremes.
- There is a strong business case recommending Trusted Teams.
- There is an equally strong human case recommending Trusted Teams.

CHAPTER 6

BUILDING A
TRUSTED TEAM

On average, we spend more waking hours with our
coworkers than we do with our families. But do they
know what we really care about? Do they understand
our values? Do they share in our triumphs and pains?

—U.S. Surgeon General Vivek Murthy[1]

How do you build a Trusted Team that values strong relationships and individual well-being? Where do you start?

Realize first that this is a living process. You are already thinking about these issues, and you've probably already taken some
first steps, but the work of maintaining a Trusted Team is never
done because business conditions are always changing. People's
life situations, their needs and contributions, are dynamic and
ever evolving.

Success comes from adopting a startup mindset. Business
startups begin with an idea, a goal, a plan, and then strive for incre-

mental progress using iterative methods like design thinking and agile development. Your purpose is to create a team that constantly builds trusted relationships and well-being as you accomplish work. This chapter gives you principles and guidelines for doing that, but bear in mind that the startup mentality is more like playing jazz than following a symphonic score. You know the theme, you are familiar with the players, and you listen to each other while you work together—but ultimately the music you make together will be uniquely your own.

Startups in business value progress over perfection. Even as notorious a perfectionist as Steve Jobs said, "Real artists ship," meaning they turn their ideas into products or services and test them in the marketplace. A bias toward action in a team works the same way: if you want to improve your team's way of working together, you have to try different ideas to build psychological safety, empathy, and trust among the members. Different people will still adopt different styles. For example, if the team leader is an extrovert Pioneer who loves talking out ideas aloud, that doesn't mean the introvert Guardians have to blue-sky ideas just as much. And the difference between those two styles doesn't compel the Integrators to smooth over conflicting styles, or the Driver on the team to stop pushing it to get the work done. It does mean that everyone can take the time to build the team dynamic that works for them . . . together.

Most of this book addresses changes you can make in your immediate surroundings—namely, your team. A startup mentality doesn't need approval from the top to be effective; in fact many far-reaching changes began as simple initiatives among team members who told each other, "There's got to be a better way to work together." That might be a formal process or an informal series of steps that humanizes and energizes a team. Think of your team as a small, very talented jazz band that's setting out to hit its goals with a bit of improvisation along the way. You'll find that some ideas work and suit your group, and you'll probably make up some of your own.

Break Barriers. Build Bridges

A startup begins with a close look at the current situation. The activities we recommended in Chapters 4 and 5, as you thought about your work style and your team's style, are a place to start. Now look at the overall landscape, and consider the structural and cultural barriers that stand in the way of progress.

Structural barriers are built-in physical, technological, and organizational walls that keep people from connecting with their full humanity. For example, large organizations can have workplaces that separate people physically, from private offices to multinational facilities. Deloitte recognized this kind of barrier when it designed Deloitte University, its leadership development center near Dallas, Texas. It is a long horizontal building, with classes, meeting spaces, a gym, a market, and other gathering spaces that were designed to create spontaneous connections among people from all over the organization, no matter their seniority or status. As employees return to post-pandemic workplaces, there will be further innovations to enable both spontaneous connections and safety.

List the structural barriers where you work, and consider which ones you want to change, whether you can change them, and how you might change them. The list might include barriers like these:

- Workplace design that separates people more than necessary. This happens with old-fashioned "everybody in your own cubicle" designs, and paradoxically, in the more recent "bench" designs that forced people together to the extent that everyone wore headphones for a bit of privacy or concentrated work.

- Virtual teams and remote work. The COVID-19 pandemic put millions of people in this situation, and a quick return to crowded office space is unlikely. Both of us worked in virtual teams long before the pandemic, and we worked with our teams to break down this structural barrier.

- Separation of teams and organizations into functional silos. This is a familiar aspect of bureaucracy. If you work in marketing, how often do you talk to someone in finance? If you work in the central office, whom do you know on the production floor? Functional separation happens in small teams too, such as the team that meets on Monday, sets its tasks, and doesn't talk again until Friday, leaving little room for informal human conversation.

- Separation of cross-functional teams into a power hierarchy, such as the "deciders" and the "doers."

- Reward systems of pay and promotion that are skewed toward an elite group, or obsolete practices like "rank-and-yank" performance reviews.

Name Your Structural Barriers

Try this team exercise: Have team members list the structural barriers in your workplace, choosing from the list above or adding their own. Then share those in open discussion, asking:

- How and/or why did each appear?
- What purpose does each serve? Did it once fulfill a purpose that is now obsolete?
- Is there a cost to continuing each (in trust, productivity, or achievement of team goals)?
- What alternative behaviors or attitudes can you imagine?

Then consider how a change in team behavior might address the cost of the barrier (there are a number of ideas for changing behavior in Part Three). Discuss both changes that you can make within your team and changes that might affect the organization at large.

Cultural barriers are the formal and informal rules of behavior that keep people from connecting or promoting well-being. For example:

- Workism—the secular "religion" that honors overwork (or its appearance) over well-being, friendship, empathy, and fun.
- Time constraint. We're all busy at times, but when busyness becomes workism, people don't build in the time to get to know their team members as people.
- Too much internal competition, proceeding from a scarcity mindset in which team members are focused on outdoing each other to win limited rewards. Those rewards might be money, prestige, promotion, or power. While those have value, the internal competition we described as the School of Sharks keeps people apart in ways that hurt productivity in the long run.
- Overreliance on email to communicate what might best be shared face-to-face or in a call. Related is indiscriminate email use, including the dreaded "Reply all."
- Always defaulting to communication apps when conversation would be more spontaneous, creative, and human.
- Myths like "We don't make friends at work" and "We don't need to have fun at work."
- Not speaking up, sharing an opinion or idea, from either personal discomfort or feelings of unease based on low status or power.
- Peoples' self-censorship based on lack of diversity, inclusion, and belonging.

Name Your Cultural Barriers

Try a team exercise similar to the previous one: Have team members
list the cultural barriers in your workplace, choosing from the list above
or adding their own. Then share those in open discussion, asking:

- How and/or why did each appear?
- What purpose does each serve? Is it aligned with your team
  values?
- Is there a cost to continuing each (in trust, productivity, or
  achievement of team goals)?
- What alternative behaviors or attitudes can you imagine?

Then consider how a change in team behavior might address the
cost of the cultural barrier (there are a number of ideas for changing
behavior in Part Three).

Safety, Empathy, and Trust

Psychological safety is a foundation of Trusted Teams. If your
team is constantly driving for results without the members taking
time to know one another, people are going to protect themselves.
They're less likely to take a risk by questioning the group consen-
sus or suggesting alternative ways to solve a problem. The result is
a limited ability to be innovative and successful because the team is
constantly driving for one particular outcome or approach, often
based on HIPPO (highest-paid person's opinion). If you don't create an environment where people feel okay sharing different points
of view, the most creative team members will learn to self-censor,
which limits everyone's creativity because nobody's taking a novel
idea and building on it.

Psychological safety doesn't mean every moment in the team is
peaceful, calm, and unpressured. It means people have learned the

skills to work through conflicting perspectives, feelings, and ideas with confidence that at the end, they will be okay. They agree that the team functions best when it surfaces and works through conflicting ideas, suggestions, and inspirations with mutual respect. (There are excellent techniques for working through differences in books like *Getting to Yes* and *Difficult Conversations.*)

Psychological safety must be deliberately established and explicitly stated in words and behavior. A team leader has to model it beyond saying, "Okay you guys, here's how we'll work out this question." It's built from many moments of respect.

For example, during a meeting the leader notices that one of the members hasn't offered any comments. Knowing that this person is temperamentally quiet, she might pull him aside or send him a note after, saying, "Corey, you've heard all the suggestions from the group. Would you like to add any ideas? And if so, we can share them in a note to the marketing team." Another way to bring everyone's voices in would be to say, "We have to have final support scripts about this product for the training group in two weeks, so they have time to train customer support. Everyone please make your suggestions by next Wednesday's meeting, either in person then or in writing to Tamara, who will organize and share them, so we can come to a final recommendation."

In both examples, the leader showed that all voices matter, that people are encouraged to state their thoughts in the way that suits them best, and that the leader cares about each individual as well as the success of the team. That leader is modeling behavior and also demonstrating a key emotional skill of Trusted Teams: empathy.

Empathy is the ability to recognize and understand other people's feelings. The empathetic person has insight into other people's motivations, the underlying reasons for their behavior and their drives and desires. Empathy recognizes emotions and connects them to behavior, and as such, it is not just emotional but analytical. It includes the ability to relate to others, to recognize ourselves in a storyline, and to trust and feel complex emotions.[2]

In business terms, customer research, design thinking, and the iterative steps of agile software development are all employing empathy to improve products and services. Regarding employees, empathetic organizations consider the "human experience" similar to how most organizations view the customer experience, according to Deloitte Digital's Amelia Dunlop. She notes that 80 percent of human decisions are driven by emotion and suggests that organizations consciously create experiences that align with people's values from beginning to end.[3]

Gallup research established four broad types of meaningful moments on teams: (1) when you propose a new idea, (2) when you ask for help, (3) when you push back on something, and (4) when you ask a personal favor. All these situations leave you vulnerable to rejection in its many forms, from being ignored to outright scorn. "The way this vulnerability is received will either build the culture or break it," wrote Gallup's Jake Herway, "and will either help or hinder both the individual's and the organization's ability to produce their best performance."[4]

Do you and your team members understand the "user experience" you are creating for yourselves? Dr. Dacher Keltner shared some of the skills that being open to other people's emotions requires: "How can you be quiet and take in the emotions of others? How can you accept hard emotions and move on? We are learning a lot about how to do that through the mindfulness and other leadership techniques. Leaders used to say, writing code or doing biotech is hard. Now we know that handling people's emotions is the hardest part of leadership."[5]

The third foundational quality of these teams is trust—a word whose meaning is much larger than it appears on first glance. We say we trust people when we have confidence that they will not lie (truthfulness), that they will do what they say (reliability) and own what they do (accountability), that they will behave consistently (steadfastness), and that they have our backs and will treat us fairly (safety).

Trust is so important to every interaction on a team that we put it in the name "Trusted Teams." Here's why: a relationship without trust can be functional only if you devote tremendous energy and time to managing the lack of trust. Imagine if you had to verify everything you team members said. You'd have no energy left to do your own work!

Trust means you rely on the fact that the people on your team will make decisions based on shared values. People understand which behaviors are acceptable and which are not; and when they stay within those behavioral guardrails, they can focus on what matters, whether that's work or each other. Bonds of trust are particularly important at the team level, where there's less sense of distance between people than, for example, between a manager and the CEO. You see this in surveys where employees feel better about their peers than about executive management, and it's not always because executives haven't earned some level of trust. It's because day in and day out, members of high-functioning Trusted Teams are exposed to each other up close. They've seen each other under stress, in failure, and in success; they've come through good times and bad together and looked out for one another's welfare. When trust is built like that, people step out of their emotional armor and build stronger bonds.

Employees in trusting cultures can focus on their work. Trust accelerates productivity because it bridges psychological divides of all kinds (age, culture, personality, etc.). When people mutually believe "we're all in this together," they put more energy into helping each other achieve common goals.

When trust is scarce, efforts to move forward together run into a wall of doubt and cynicism. In the worst cultures, lack of trust creates nonstop conflict among different factions—an elite (and allies) versus everyone else. And trust quickly dies when people do something different from what they commit to, or don't hold themselves to the same standards they demand of others.

If this all seems elementary—it is!

Think of an organization you've known where trust was part of the culture. Leadership earned the trust of other employees, managers trusted their staffs to do the right thing, and teams could count on each other to tell the truth and follow up on their commitments. Now compare it with one where that wasn't the case (and if you have no comparison company, think of another situation like a dysfunctional committee you've served on or even a family you've known). Consider how much energy gets spent compensating for lack of trust, and how much better that energy could be put to use.

Trust is a nonnegotiable component of a team with strong relationships and strong well-being.

DEEP Principles at Sanofi

Roberto Pucci, chief human resource officer (CHRO) of global pharmaceutical company Sanofi, shared his principles for leadership in conversations with Deloitte:

> We really push what we call the DEEP principles of leadership conversations: being Direct, Empathetic, Earnest and Productive. To make a person feel comfortable, you need to be Direct. A conversation needs to be candid and open, not two-faced. Second, be Empathetic. Being emotionally intelligent shows the person in front of you that you can connect with them not just rationally, but also emotionally. The third dimension is being Earnest, which means being honest and working to deliberately create trust. Finally, it's important to make each conversation Productive: Give a sense of optimism to the person you are talking to. Show there is light at the end of the tunnel.[6]

Choose Your Team's Values

Psychologist Edgar Schein proposed a classic model for understanding organizational culture, and it's a useful perspective for looking at your team. Schein said a culture is realized on three levels: artifacts, espoused values, and basic assumptions:

> *Artifacts* are visible and obvious parts of an organization, including the organizations's physical environment and its norms of dress, language and behavior. You can think of Wall Street's bespoke suits and Silicon Valley's hoodies as artifacts.
>
> *Espoused values* are those principles we see in mission statements, branding, slogans, and annual reports—the public face of what an organization stands for.
>
> *Shared basic assumptions* are the beliefs and values that are the "dogma" or core beliefs of an organization. It's this third level that forms the daily experience of employees and tests the truthfulness of the other two levels.[7]

As a member of an organization, you might have some limited influence on artifacts and espoused values. As a member of a team, you have more influence on shared basic assumptions by choosing how you will treat each other. Trusted Teams translate shared basic assumptions into behavior, and this cannot be left to chance. How to act out your values must be an ongoing conversation among team members for the simple reason that business confronts anyone with dozens of opportunities every day to behave in conformity with agreed values or to violate them.

Imagine these moments:

- A client calls, angry because part of a project is late. The person was yelled at by his boss, and now he wants to share the pain. How you handle the next few minutes on the phone tests team values like accountability, customer focus, and shared responsibility. Are you defensive or empathetic?

- A team member made a key suggestion in a casual conversation that improved some part of a project. Do you share credit?
- A deadline is closing in and your part of a collaboration is "good enough" but not great. You're not sure how to make it great . . . and that deadline is coming closer. What do you do— admit your doubts or stay quiet and hope for the best?
- Someone's outspokenness in meetings bothers you, or someone's inability to get to the point drives you crazy. How do you handle it?

We'd like to see all organizations embrace the values of strong relationships and well-being. Leadership is responsible for promoting them in espoused values and shared basic assumptions, but even when that happens in an organization, it's up to people at the team level to make relationships and well-being a reality.

Anh's team has worked to maintain a startup mentality while also building psychological safety, empathy, and trust. The team members are passionate about what they do and passionate about supporting each other. We'll use them as an example of a team in the process of combining strong relationships and well-being practices.

The team consists of 6 to 8 core members and an extended team of 12 to 15 "members of the community" who join on an as-needed basis. They sit in the emerging tech group of Deloitte Consulting, LLP, reporting to the chief technology officer. Their job is to collaborate with other parts of the organization to conduct and publish research on emerging technology trends and technology leadership topics.

A team taking on temporary additions and working on fast-paced technology research can't have ironclad roles and responsibilities. Nobody says "Not my job" when on a project. People's roles blur as one person takes responsibility for a certain phase of a project, while another steps in to manage a parallel phase or a different project. At any given time, someone could be heading up one initiative while just supporting and contributing to another. While the team strives to have its people dedicate most of their time to the things they do best, no responsibility is formally too large or too small for anyone. The most junior person on the team is able to contribute to big-picture thinking and comment on strategy. When speed and quality are equally important on a project, work gets allocated to the best available person, requiring regular balancing and directing of resources.

The team has to be flexible and adaptable to changing conditions, which is emblematic of startups. Contrast this with rigid bureaucracies that operate like a giant machine, with the individual participants acting predictably in their specialized function.

"It sounds ambiguous," says Anh, "but we work fine this way because we have agreed on ways of working that guide us. We started by committing to one another that every person on the team is helping to shape our culture, for good or bad. People forget that they have a role in reinforcing their culture."

Last year the team collaborated to establish Ways of Working principles, which are depicted in Figure 6.1. Everyone on the team contributed to the principles. They guide the team's style of work toward the values that make a Trusted Team.

Ways of Working reminds team members to be deliberate in their work when simple inertia or overwhelming busyness tempts them to do things the easy/familiar/expedient way. It's a living set of principles that the members of the team discuss as part of doing great work while taking care of each other. Some principles, like "Remain hyperfocused on quality, impact, and mission," have obvious meaning, and the team periodically considers the other principles.

Ways of Working—Outcome Not Activity

Think and behave like a startup (the startup way)
Remain hyperfocused on quality, impact, and mission
Adopt agile mindset, behaviors, and processes—sprint, iterative delivery
Always be in beta; find ways to work smarter, rather than just harder
Be curious; embrace a culture of learning
Develop depth and expertise
Push outside your comfort zone and swim lane
Learn to prioritize; be OK with saying "No"; focus by sacrificing for the good of the great

FIGURE 6.1 Agreed-upon principles guide the team's work.

"Think and behave like a startup" borrows concepts from agile development and design thinking. The team members focus on collaborative and iterative ways of working. And they value people, interactions, outcomes, collaboration, and responsiveness over rigid and inflexible tools, processes, and plans.

"Always be in beta" means be alert to how any process can be improved. As a research organization, we're open to many different ways to acquire and analyze information about topics. The same is true of our own work. A related idea is that we learn to say no to the idea of perfection. Perfectionism leads to paralysis; it creates a habit of saying "I'm not ready yet."

"Focus by sacrificing the good for the great" means that along the way to a goal, we'll have lots of good ideas that just don't belong in the final product. We all get attached to our brainstorms—the bit of research we love; the extra code we write; the new feature that's so cool it just has to be in the product. At work, we strive for the same simplicity displayed by great artists, athletes, business thinkers, and other exceptional practitioners. We focus and simplify.

"Be curious" and "Develop depth and expertise" are habits that help us continuously improve. It's part of our passion for well-being that everyone on the team continues to grow. If someone outgrows the team and moves to another group, we will miss the person, but we take it as one sign that the group is succeeding. When the team discusses research or new ways of doing things, people get curious about each other's discoveries. "What does that mean?" and "Tell me more about that" are frequent parts of our discussions.

The team also worked out Everyday Equations, which are principles that guide decision making. Everyday Equations are deliberate choices between competing values. It's a concept made popular by Deloitte Consulting LLP's CEO Dan Helfrich, and the team came up with its own set of equations, shown in Figure 6.2. The current draft list (it can change and grow over time) shows which alternative values must be ranked and which alternatives must be balanced as equally important.

What Are Our Everyday Equations?

People > processes

Outcomes > activities

Giving opportunity > guaranteeing success

Shared success = individual success

Today's win > tomorrow's tasks

Well-being = priority #1

Balanced progress > chaotic/stressful productivity

Dreaming big = taking many small steps

Moving forward > moving perfectly

Radical Candor > being "nice"

FIGURE 6.2 Everyday Equations: choosing among competing values.

Take, for example, the equation "Well-being = priority #1." It's priority #1 the team agrees, because without well-being, all the other choices will take place in the context of a stressed-out team that is less effective and less happy than it could be. In the equation "Shared success = individual success," reminds us that our best performance is based on teamwork; and "Dreaming big = taking many small steps" means that dreaming big is just as important as (but not more important than) taking many small steps to get there.

"People > processes" says that people are more important than processes, which translates into team members supporting each other by staying flexible in the way they accomplish work. When people stepped up during the pandemic to help the single mom navigate working from home, that was putting people before processes. Equally important is the equation "Giving opportunity > guaranteeing success." Giving someone an opportunity to try something new, though there's no guarantee of success, is a great way to stretch each member of the team. People grow when given opportunity, and the capacity of the team to do more quality work grows with them.

"Radical Candor," a work technique described in Kim Scott's insightful book of the same name, means the members of the team simultaneously care personally about each other and directly challenge problems, ideas, behaviors, or beliefs with which they disagree. To engage in a conflict of ideas with an attitude of compassion and respect for one another is a test of a team's maturity; it also happens to be a superb way to work through difficulties.

"Balanced progress > chaotic/stressful productivity" acknowledges that we are all habituated to constant activity, but also asserts that isn't how we get to good outcomes over time. Instead, we get burned out trying to do everything. One feature of high-functioning teams is that they always come up with more cool ideas than they have capacity to realize. In order to be effective, they have to make steady progress on the things that count most. This equation is another reminder that focus and choosing to say no are necessary for progress.

And on a related note: "Moving forward > moving perfectly" is another warning against perfectionism. "Paralysis by analysis," "The perfect is the enemy of the good," and "Progress, not perfection" are time-tested slogans that speak to the powerful human desire to get it perfect. That's impossible over time because there is no permanent, fixed state of perfection in business.

Trusted Teams use other tools in the spirit of continuous growth. Active listening, when you stay silent and then clarify what someone has said ("Let me see if I understand . . ."), is a proven way for teams to share knowledge and bypass groupthink. Distributed leadership for projects exposes people to decision making and resource allocation. Diversity on a team, including diversity of thought, encourages creativity and innovation. Even in our small teams, we think about enabling diverse connections with the rest of the company. We tell our teammates, "If everyone you come in contact with at work looks like you, thinks like you, has the same opinions as you, you need to get out more." Think about bringing some contrasting experiences and opinions into your work. Share your ideas with someone who comes from a different background, country, or discipline. Find out about these others and their work—it will enrich yours. It's not easy for a virtual team to do this, and it's especially difficult during times like the pandemic when people work from home, but it can be done. In fact, you might be assuming it's harder than it is because you're so used to communicating via email or through collaboration platforms with just your team that you forget you can pick up the phone or set a time to talk with that person you saw contributing to the company's social media feed.

Putting Positivity into Action

In Chapter 5, we cited research demonstrating that positive teams are more productive. That research found that positive practices in companies are best implemented in four ways. First, leadership has to model the practices. Second, culture change initiatives should focus on personal actions like recognizing people for the things they do well (as opposed to just noting things that must change). A third factor is a focus on small, attainable actions like keeping gratitude journals or practicing meditation. The fourth factor is conducting retreats, but not the usual corporate strategy or management retreats. Instead, workshops emphasizing positive leadership skills like appreciation and connectedness were found to increase positivity and productivity.[8]

More Ways to Strengthen Relationships

In addition to conscious decisions like Ways of Working and Everyday Equations, we've observed a number of ways teams can strengthen relationships in the course of work. Performance management, promotions, common goals, and collaboration tech are good ways to strengthen Trusted Teams.

Performance management is so much more than giving each employee an annual review. When managers move from being judges to becoming coaches, the whole perspective shifts from "rating" to "growing" every employee. Feedback should be frequent, positive, and instructive. Simple techniques like reflective listening and feedback analysis help people grow themselves. Modern social recognition programs, which enable everyone to encourage and coach everyone else, are effective ways not only to manage performance but also to increase employee engagement, loyalty, and satisfaction.

You also want to connect performance to more than individual contribution. Just as sophisticated compensation programs recognize individual and group performance, so people can be coached and incentivized to contribute to team performance. The best performers we know also make the people around them better.

Consider the contrast between the US Olympic ice-skating team and the US Olympic hockey team. While the figure skaters represent the same country and connect on a certain social and professional level, they are in the end also competing against one another. Ultimately, individual performance is the center of everyone's career. Maybe your team should be a little bit more like a hockey team (or in our families, a soccer team) where each player on the team is working together with everyone else on the team to achieve a common goal. The interdependent business team needs to fully reward and recognize not just the person who makes the goal but also the one who makes the assist. It's not only the shot makers but the defense that wins the game, and that's much more like a work team.

We've talked about the distancing effect of workplace technology, but the embedding of tech into every part of our work lives is a great thing if we use it mindfully. So we'll note here that using collaboration tools can strengthen relationships as well: They enable frequent, informal conversation. They're good for quick knowledge sharing or decision making that doesn't require a meeting. They are built to handle changing conditions. And they allow team members to engage, disengage, or reengage more smoothly than traditional email.

But "mindfully" is the most important word in the previous paragraph. Apps that work on the same stimulus-response mechanisms in our brains need to be tempered with the discipline to resist interruption. Teams should set rules that separate the important work from the urgent-but-unimportant trap that timeline-based apps set.

Both of us put a lot of effort into being aware of our automatic response to email, and we'd bet most of you do as well. Do you use email like an uncontrolled taskmaster would, to constantly send out both things that you need other people to do and commitments to work you'll accomplish by such and such a time? Do you habitually act on the impulse that says, "This'll only take a minute; might as well get it out of my inbox"? Are you sending emails at 2 a.m. on a Thursday or 1 p.m. on a Sunday and setting the example that this is what you expect your team to do? (A friend recalls an email thread among five people in three states at 11 p.m., which devolved into a discussion about how late everyone was working, which then turned into a conversation about how habitual this was—but nobody felt empowered to just leave the email thread until the boss did.)

What about traditional social events at work—mixers, parties, and similar events? Research tells us that most people don't create meaningful connections at social events related to work. The problem with mixers is that people don't actually mix. They hang out with friends or colleagues they already know or do big-group activities. Solid social connections are more likely to happen in small, informal activities like playing Jenga or taking a walk outside (and yes, that means the Ping-Pong and pool tables can stay).

Model and Promote Well-Being

Part Three of this book shows things you can do for your own well-being and ways to build a Trusted Team where everyone looks out for everyone else's well-being. When well-being is a way of work for everyone, the whole organization becomes stronger, as outcomes in health and productivity (and all the components of those big domains) improve.

Anh and her team put well-being at the top of their list of Everyday Equations because Trusted Team members look out for each other's individual health and happiness. They are passionate about supporting one another and understand that every individual has a unique path to fulfillment at work.

Like the work of building strong relationships, the work of well-being is a process that has a beginning but no end. It too is more like playing jazz than a symphony score, because what makes for well-being at one stage of life or career might change. Also, what people need to improve their well-being is individual.

Imagine a person in top physical shape who spends early morning and all weekend training for the next marathon. Now imagine how that intensity translates into work habits—obsessively checking emails when she gets up at 5 a.m. and texting the work team on Saturday night about the next week's projects. Now imagine the recipient of that text is a person who meditates, leaves work at work, and is trying to break the habit of checking emails first thing in the morning. Add a third member of the team, who is physically healthy and projects a sunny attitude, but is consumed with anxiety over his growing (and secret) credit card debt. Different well-being issues call for different solutions.

Well-being works best when top-down support meets grass roots, just like building a culture of strong relationships. Jen keeps an updated list of the many big and small actions that promote well-being, and how people at any level of the organization can participate. People from many companies and countries have contributed to the list, and so it's inclusive of a great number of work situations.

Three major themes emerge as we talk to employees about their well-being experiences. First, people desire work that is both conducive for well-being and reflective of a culture that encourages (or even requires) employees to engage in well-being actions—for both themselves and others. Second, people would like their organizations to offer flexible work schedules and permission to dedicate time to individual well-being during work. Third, people are seeking more time to connect with colleagues and opportunities to share how they are doing from a well-being standpoint.

Here are steps that can be undertaken at different levels of influence and authority:

Leaders

- Model and support well-being yourselves; walk the talk by taking time off, joining employees in physical and mental health activities; elevate well-being initiatives at company meetings and communications.
- Connect to all aspects of the workforce experience, meaning physical space, recreational activities, and the all-important connection between espoused values and leadership behavior.
- Train managers and supervisors and monitor behaviors and results—well-being work and its effects can and should be measured regularly through surveys and check-ins.
- Build well-being deliverables and results into your performance management system.
- Understand the well-being support, programs, and interventions available to your organization by keeping up with its growing literature and management ideas.
- Allow for activities specifically designed for well-being as part of the work environment/schedule.
- Include well-being training for managers and other employees in corporate development budgets.

Managers

- Model well-being behaviors such as email blackout times.
- Discuss worker well-being needs and challenges.
- Understand the well-being support, programs, and interventions available.
- Solicit input on roles and design of workspace, technology, and routines.
- Connect well-being steps to mission and values.
- Set clear expectations and goals, prioritize work, and establish norms for team meetings, assignments, and adaptation to changing conditions.
- Encourage time to disconnect.
- Understand worker strengths and assign work based on strengths and work styles. Actively manage and adjust work distribution and workloads.
- Make well-being activities part of performance management discussions.
- Create and allow for social connection.

All Employees

- Communicate well-being needs and challenges.
- Identify flex scheduling requests and communicate personal commitments.
- Give input into the design of work.
- Set boundaries.
- Build social connections.
- Practice self-care.
- Disconnect.
- Take breaks.

What If You're Not in Charge?

A culture of well-being begins at the top, with senior leadership modeling the behaviors and beliefs that support well-being.

But what if that leadership isn't yet supporting the message, and you're not in charge?

We need to give ourselves permission to take the steps necessary to protect our physical, mental, financial well-being, and a sense of purpose. And too often we don't do that. Jen admits that not giving herself permission to take care led to her burnout (and subsequent career change). Leaders play a critical role, but we're all responsible for creating the culture we want to work in!

Creating a culture works best if it's both top down and bottom up, so if you're not in charge, you can start at the grass roots. Find allies who have the same values around relationships and well-being and begin an ongoing conversation about what changes you have the collective power to make.

You (alone or with others) can speak directly with the leader of your team, department, or company about having regular check-ins as part of the routine. Point out the business benefits we've explained above. You might make a connection that people hadn't seen between leadership-level concerns like employee engagement on the one hand and the practice of well-being and the building of strong relationships on the other.

If you're a manager, you can influence your peers and people on your team who might not have considered the importance of these. People get so used to the way things are, and so focused on the next to-do item, that they don't imagine a different way of working. If relationships and well-being are important to you, they'll be important to other people, and your willingness to start a conversation, to stick with the conversation, might be the motivation for others to help you make the change you envision.

Kindness: The Well-Being Accelerator

If psychological safety, empathy, and trust still seem unlikely to you in a work situation, Dr. Kelli Harding poses a powerful argument in their favor. The Columbia University psychologist and author of *The Rabbit Effect* spoke to Jen recently about how love, friendship, community, purpose, and our environment affect our health more than what happens in a doctor's office.

"We know that mental health costs over a trillion dollars a year in lost productivity; yet oftentimes there's still a stigma around it," Dr. Harding told Jen during a Deloitte *WorkWell* podcast. "I think [the problem] is like where we were in the 1930s with smoking. It was everywhere, but nobody could figure out what was causing all these problems."

Dr. Harding continued, noting that "micro-kindnesses" at work offer an achievable way to ease the problem in the workplace: "It's little things; it's like when you walk down the hall to go grab a cup of water, you pause to look people in the eyes, saying hello. We know that when it comes to our social circles, both quality and quantity matter, and that means those little micro-interactions really count.

"Being kind is good, and then also receiving kindness is good. And I think it is really important to know that giving the kindness and whoever you are, that's an important part of being a human being, and it boosts our health. It boosts our immune system, lowers our blood pressure, and helps us feel better. . . . There are large population studies showing that our workplaces have a profound impact on our health, and most of us think that it's important to have a good doctor, but it turns out it's also important [to our health] to have a good manager."

Jen's experience as a breast cancer survivor is informative. She recounts, "I was very fortunate that I had this work community to support me. Once you're done with treatment, you're not seeing your doctors regularly. People stop checking in, not because they're ill-intentioned, but because everybody is excited that you're done with treatment and life goes back to some sort of new normal."

She concludes: "I advise people in a supportive role to continue those check-ins with survivors, or anyone recovering from adversity, whether that's physical or emotional. Sometimes that aftermath is the hardest part, because survivors can live with a residual fear—"What if it comes back?"

At times like that, when the world has been upended, small acts of kindness are invaluable. They are the ultimate bridge across the chasm of our overscheduled, overproductive, and overtechnically enhanced lives. Human to human, kindness of all kinds affirms our importance to each other. Who wouldn't want to belong to a team like that?

What the COVID-19 Pandemic Might Change for Well-Being

In April 2020 Tracy Brower, author of *Bring Work to Life by Bringing Life to Work,* offered predictions for the post-COVID-19 workplace. These items caught our notice as being directly tied to well-being:

- Support for mental health will expand, with special attention paid to alleviating isolation caused by social distancing and remote work.
- More companies will acknowledge the importance of culture as a context for performance, rather than leaving culture to chance.
- Having weathered a crisis together, employees will preserve the stronger social bonds they established, continuing to support each other as face-to-face work returns.

- Managers and peers will have greater empathy for the demands of life outside of work, such as family responsibilities. "They will have a refreshed appreciation for the ways family and friends are critical to life and happiness."[9]

We are noticing similar and other changes that contribute to both individual well-being and corporate survival, such as companies buying equipment for ergonomic home offices.

We believe that the sum of these and other changes will be a more flexible, technology-enhanced, and innovative attitude toward how work gets done. A crisis focuses the attention of both individuals and teams, enabling them to discard unnecessary habits and attitudes. Preserving the status quo, appearing invulnerable, leaving your personal life at the door—we have an opportunity to discard these cultural artifacts and create a more humane, empathetic, and human workplace. At the same time, we can discover that our shared humanity and care for each other makes us more productive, innovative, and competitive in the marketplace.

KEY POINTS

- Building a Trusted Team begins with recognizing and dealing with structural and cultural barriers to change.
- Safety, empathy, and trust are elementary, and must be deliberately grown and nurtured as part of teamwork.
- Write your team's Ways of Working and Everyday Equations as a way to design and build a Trusted Team.
- Model and promote well-being with practical steps as well as kindness and compassion for each other.

PART THREE

PEOPLE FIRST, SYSTEMS SECOND

P art Three is about why well-being matters and the skills and habits employees need to design it into their work.

"People First, Systems Second" is about developing an awareness of all the systems affecting our work (technology, organizational hierarchy, culture, personal habits) and modifying those systems to serve the health of our bodies, minds, and businesses. We love technology and depend on systems, but organizational inertia exaggerates their influence for good or ill. We need people to develop a mindful and deliberate approach to the systems around them. The good news is that when you put humans first, the systems get better as well. People are more engaged and energetic. Teams are more productive. Business priorities become more inclusive and sustainable for the simple reason that the organization isn't burning them out.

In Chapters 7 and 8, we'll show why well-being matters to individuals and businesses. We'll outline a personal well-being program and dive deeper into creating and maintaining strong relationships at work.

Chapter 9 addresses the well-being and relationship issues that have become acute with the integration of technology in every part of our lives, and the particular issues surrounding remote work and virtual environments. The inexorable growth of the virtual workplace was already happening when the COVID-19 pandemic accelerated that growth faster than anyone anticipated; and even as the pandemic comes under control, we will likely not return fully to the pre-2020 way of working. We must adjust our thinking and our work habits to thrive in the virtual workplace.

In Chapter 10 we'll lay out the principles and methods that leaders can use to weave well-being and healthy relationships into the culture of their organizations. While Trusted Teams are the place where most practical change takes place, this is a cultural change, and to be successful, it needs a change management process initiated and sustained by leadership at every level.

CHAPTER 7

PUTTING WELL-BEING INTO ACTION

Research finds that the number one regret for 76% of people is "not living my ideal self." In order to be really successful at work, you need to be really successful in your personal life. There's just no line between work and life.

—Ben Nemtin, bestselling author and star of the show *The Buried Life*

In Part Two we presented the business case and the human case for Trusted Teams. Well-being is a responsibility of good corporate citizenship and also a performance strategy. It drives employee engagement, organizational energy, and productivity.[1] It's a growing expectation among the most sought-after employees, even if they don't use exactly that term. They expect a culture in which they can do their best work and live a healthy, purposeful life. The question isn't whether well-being should be part of a culture, but how can individuals and organizations get there?

Jen: Building a Well-Being Program

When we started Deloitte's well-being programs in 2015, the first task was to help employees understand what well-being is and why it mattered to them personally. Designing well-being into daily work is a long-term process, not a brief initiative, and that requires a clear, shared definition of the concept. We created a framework around well-being, with language that communicates the benefits to people personally and professionally. It was not something we had talked about previously in any comprehensive way. Well-being is more a way of working—and a way of life—than a "job benefit" in the traditional sense.

Well-being in an organization encompasses a diverse set of programs and behaviors with a positive impact on employees' physical, mental, emotional, and financial health. It also promotes social health because teams and organizations are miniature societies. When you broaden that to include all the other relationships that touch on work, such as interactions with customers and the communities where we work, well-being has a positive effect on our professions' purpose and meaning.[2]

At Deloitte we speak of "empowered well-being" that includes body, mind, financial health, and purpose. We recognize that all the dimensions of well-being touch each other. You can't have optimum physical well-being without mental and emotional well-being. A sense of shared purpose among employees, the belief that we're all in this together, encourages us to care for each other and for ourselves. We recognize that well-being, while grounded in different activities for different people, has a common effect on employees. Well-being is a foundation for how you show up as your best self as both an employee and a person, meaning your work, values, health, and purpose are in harmony. Even in stressful times, you have a sense of ease and energetic engagement, because your work and health (in every sense of the word) are aligned.

We emphasize the need to design well-being directly into the flow of people's jobs because the inertia of work habits is powerful. We've seen well-being programs begin with great enthusiasm, as employees experiment with new work habits like those we described in Anh's group. But without sustained change, old habits creep into our work lives—after all, most of us have spent many years acquiring them! Sustained change happens when well-being informs the way work itself is designed, rather than an adjacent program of recovering from the work habits and stresses that make us unwell.

Barriers to Well-Being

There is no single template that guarantees well-being for everyone, because just as we saw with temperaments, the factors that matter are different for each person, and might change over time as circumstances and priorities at work and life change. There are, however, definite barriers to well-being, and they are often embedded so completely into the workplace that they are taken for granted.

The barriers to well-being are sometimes obvious, for example, an unfriendly culture, abusive bosses, unfair compensation or promotion actions, or a physically dangerous work environment. At both an organizational and an individual scale, however, we see the chief barriers to well-being as more subtle. They manifest as shared basic assumptions that quietly damage well-being. Many of them are products of the workism mindset we described earlier. Resistance to self-care manifests itself in many guises, among which are:

A limited definition of well-being. Well-being isn't limited to physical and mental health. Because it includes feelings of purpose and meaning, of personal significance, it is an individual and subjective state. It's more than physical health. It's more than feeling comfortable or satisfied. Sometimes people find their greatest sense of well-being when facing moments of stress or doing difficult jobs or confronting painful circumstances, provided they are authentically living their values.

A limited and strictly quantified definition of success. Workism is obsessed with measurement—how many emails sent, how much money earned, how many people reporting to you, how fast you rise up the ladder. Modern culture, in particular, associates greater material wealth with greater well-being. But ancient wisdom and modern scientific research show that after a certain level of wealth, a sense of well-being plateaus or even declines.[3] While measurement is indispensable for management, well-being is difficult to measure except by its positive effects (such as reduced sick time, less turnover, and greater employee engagement).

The idea that needing rest and recovery indicates weakness. Endurance is the currency of workism, expressed in sayings like "Just suck it up" and "Deal with it." People internalize these messages and become more focused on appearances than results, putting in long hours when they're not necessary or monitoring how quickly they empty their in-boxes instead of how effectively they're focusing on things that count. Rest and recovery are critical components of resilience, and thus essential to long-term productivity. Put simply, endurance is about spending down your capacity to work until there's nothing left; resilience is about replenishing your capacity to work by practicing rest and renewal.

The idea that burnout is the price of success. The notion that burnout is the price of success is stubbornly embedded in certain cultures and bureaucracies (Wall Street and Silicon Valley come to mind). It can produce tangible rewards like money and power even as organizations burn and churn talented employees. If you work in such an organization, you can accept the price, try to change the culture, or leave. The human cost is great, and yes, the rewards can be substantial. The real tragedy happens when people embrace this notion for years only to discover they've betrayed their own values. If you find yourself burning out for a job or culture you don't believe in, be honest about the price of that trade-off.

The idea that passion will protect from burnout. For decades people have been told to follow their passions for a more fulfilling work life. Do what you love, says the myth, and you will find boundless energy and fulfillment. The facts say otherwise: 87 percent of professionals in a recent survey say they have passion for their current job, but 64 percent say they are frequently stressed. Loving work doesn't make someone immune from burnout.[4]

The Scarcity Mindset

In 2016 Deloitte published an article on scarcity mindset: "Does Scarcity Make You Dumb?"[5] Behavioral science research suggests humans have a finite capacity for making good decisions, and scarcity of resources can diminish that capacity. The scarce resource in decision making is often time, that is, a sense that time is running out to make a decision, or that too many decisions have to be made in a limited amount of time. When this happens, an exaggerated sense of urgency can cause people to block out critical information in the rush to decide.

Management experts like Stephen Covey and President Dwight D. Eisenhower spoke of the need to distinguish between the urgent but unimportant task and the important but not urgent task. A familiar example of our mental "urgency trap" is the momentary impulse to check email, interrupting more significant work. As we noted in Chapter 1, such mental interruptions typically waste 20 minutes of productive work time. Physical interruptions, such as a coworker stopping by to ask a question, have a similar effect, and this constant start-and-stop feeds a sense of scarcity. There's never enough time because our sense of urgency spends down time on less-important work.

The scarcity article noted, "Nearly everyone suffers time crunches, but time is only one source of scarcity—attention deficits may come from a lack of money, collaboration, food, companionship, or any other valuable resource. Scarcity can be a hidden distractor that constantly pulls cognition away from other important but less urgent needs. Scarcity compromises a person's decision-making capabilities by depleting [our] finite capacity for self-control and intelligence. When [we make] bad choices, it doesn't necessarily indicate incompetence. Rather, circumstances may have exhausted [our] overall capability, creating a nearly impossible setting for making rational choices."

Scarcity wreaks havoc on our minds by constantly interrupting our thinking, by creating an intense focus on an unmet (and possibly unimportant) need, and by exhausting the mind with constant trade-off decisions.

That third effect—constant trade-offs—is a significant barrier to well-being. If you do not distinguish between the momentary gratification of answering an urgent-but-unimportant email and the longer task of drafting an important-but-not-urgent proposal, your mind undergoes a kind of temporary burnout and you become incapable of focusing on the work that matters. We've observed other kinds of self-deception such as the "planning fallacy" in which we convince ourselves that a particular task will take less time in the future than it does now (a management version of wishful thinking that might be quite unconscious). Or the "confirmation bias" in which we pay more attention to evidence that confirms our beliefs and ignore evidence that contradicts them. These are subtle ways trying to cram more tasks into less time rather than giving the thoughtful tasks most of our mental energy.

The antidote for a scarcity mindset is found in building both mindfulness and slack into the workday. Mindfulness in this context means catching time-wasting habits (like checking email) and channeling those tasks into focused or regularly scheduled times. When you can ask, "Is this the most important thing I can be doing at this moment?" and answer yes, you interrupt that unconscious sense of urgency and can take a moment to refocus on what matters most.

"Slack" might carry negative connotations to some ("He's such a slacker"), but here it means planned breaks from intense work into the day. Time positioned as a buffer between demanding tasks renews the mind's ability to engage a new task. Small changes to a schedule can add up to create a big impact, and our study suggested five ways to create slack in your day:[6]

- *Start your day off right.* Take the time to define and prioritize your daily goals and refer to those goals throughout the day to ensure alignment.
- *Create meeting buffers.* Reduce meeting times to 25 or 50 minutes to create time to reset before moving onto the next meeting or task.
- *Schedule focused work time.* During this time, turn off your email and your phone so that you can give your full attention to the task at hand.

- *Take breaks.* Schedule time to mentally recover. This means stepping away from your work to get up and move around or practice deep breathing to center yourself.
- *Schedule quiet time.* Regular pauses for quiet meditation or breathing exercises can provide a wide array of mental and physical benefits.

You can't control every minute at work. There will be times when interruptions are both urgent and important, and periods when work-life integration includes more work than life. But learning to be mindful, deliberate, and realistic about work, and building in slack to your overall schedule, builds your capacity to thrive even through the most stressful times, and gives you the resilience to reestablish an equilibrium between work and life quickly.

Make a Personal Plan

Wherever your organization is in terms of a well-being strategy, your own well-being begins with defining personal goals and planning how you will apply them to the demands of your job and your life.

It helps to be specific in your goals, whether they concern physical, mental, financial, or social well-being. What does well-being mean to you? Is it that you practice yoga twice a week, or make the time to get to the neighborhood book club or your child's soccer game? Is it achieving greater physical health, for example, reaching a weight goal, eating better, getting more exercise, or improving your sleep habits? Do you want to invest more time in personal connections with your family, church, club, or community? Your goals can begin broadly with statements like "Add community service to my life" and then become more specific with intentions like "Serve dinner to guests at the food bank twice a month."

A set of personal well-being goals needn't be overwhelming, and you don't have to change every aspect of your work and life at once. One of the most powerful techniques for success is to act on small goals that you can easily integrate into your current routine, and stick to them. Sticking to healthy activities and rituals, even small ones, provides a sense of normality that day by day gives you a feeling of control as well as progress. Achieving micro-goals has the added benefit of building a sense of awareness and mindfulness about your daily schedule and moment-by-moment routines. If you pause twice a day for a five-minute breathing exercise, that's twice a day you're less likely to get swept away into email or other messages. Small changes can counteract the scarcity mindset.

Here are places to start:[7]

- *Eat a nutritious meal or snack every two to three hours.* Eating light and eating often gives your body just the right amount of fuel, which helps to improve energy levels, brain function, and mood.
- *Keep a water bottle or glass with you to stay hydrated while you work.*
- *Move more.* We've heard it said that sitting is the new smoking. Try to stand up at your workspace frequently or during a call. Doing chair exercises or using resistance bands or a balance ball, if you have one, can offset some of the effects of sitting.
- *Get some exercise!* Stepping outside for a walk and some fresh air does both your mind and body good. There are also many videos on the internet featuring stretching, yoga, and other workouts you can easily do in your living room, whatever your fitness level.
- *Try meditation.* Scientific studies confirm that meditation is an effective way to manage stress and practice mindfulness. There are several meditation apps that make it easy to get

started. You can also try just taking a few deep breaths—inhaling for a few seconds, holding it, and then slowly exhaling. Or try thinking about three to five things you're grateful for every time you wash your hands.

- *Schedule breaks in your calendar.* When working remotely, there aren't those natural breaks in the day that you might have had before, such as a commute. Think about using the time that you might have had for your commute to exercise or to meditate. You can also take a quick joy break to watch a favorite video or listen to your favorite song while dancing.

Sleep deserves an honored position in your routine; it has beneficial effects on memory, the immune system, learning, and other physical and mental functions.[8] To really recharge and refresh your mind and body, as an adult you need seven to nine hours of sleep,[9] so create a nighttime sleep ritual that makes getting those hours a priority:

- Make your bedroom a screen-free zone so that the blue light from your devices doesn't interfere with your ability to fall asleep.
- Turn off notifications from devices, including phones, during sleep hours. You can leave the ringer on to wake you in an emergency.
- Exercise during the day—it can promote more and healthier sleep.
- If you have medical issues with sleep, such as insomnia or sleep apnea, talk to your doctor. Every night you don't deal with these medical issues is a lost chance to perform well inside and outside of work.
- Get outside or near a window. There's evidence that exposure to natural light in the morning helps regulate your sleep cycle.

- Limit caffeine according to your personal tolerance, in both how much you consume and how late in the day you have it.
- Moderate alcohol intake. Alcohol can make you feel sleepy at first, but more than a moderate amount interferes with the deep-sleep cycle.[10]

Rest and recovery go beyond sleep. Give yourself permission to slow down and connect with a deeper part of yourself, in the ways suggested above or any other way that works for you. When we stop all the busyness for even a short time, we can get clarity on what we need to do to feel better about ourselves, no matter the transient circumstances.

Small Steps Lead to Big Changes

Sometimes the biggest barrier to self-care is feeling like it's too much to plan or there isn't enough time. To make it easier, try breaking well-being activities down into small steps. Choose one thing to add to your routine and then build from there. For example, if you're determined to eat more healthy food, start with three meals a week. To simplify it, pick the same meal—say, eating a balanced breakfast on Monday, Wednesday, and Friday. You can plan to have wholesome food in the house on those days, and for those three times a week, either have it ready in the fridge or get up 15 minutes earlier to prepare breakfast. You can still stop at the bagel shop on Tuesday or Thursday if you like, but as the new habit becomes routine, you'll feel good about the improvement in your eating habits. Then you add two healthy lunches a week, and so on.

Using this snowball approach, you can gradually build momentum, and before long, you'll have added several healthy habits to your daily routine. And your chances of developing longer-term well-being are much greater than trying to tackle a big life change all at once.

Small steps are also the way to realign your relationship to technology, a topic we'll address in Chapter 9.

To help you make these healthy habits a part of your daily routine, you may want to try putting them on your calendar, just like you would any meeting or phone call. If you were to look at our calendars right now, you would see recurring appointments for breakfast, lunch, dinner, time for movement or exercise, and even bedtime. Placing even ordinary breaks on the calendar helps us honor these commitments. And sharing this information helps groups like Anh's preserve their promise to make well-being priority #1.

As you add healthy habits, consider whether it's time to let go of a few things as well. During the pandemic, Jen went back to her to-do list and crossed off several intentions that just weren't useful or relevant anymore. Putting those aside created psychological room to embrace her new habits with enthusiasm.

Psychological Well-Being

In *The Transformation Myth*,[11] the authors study how leaders adapted to the sudden new world of remote work, widespread unemployment, disrupted supply chains, and new routines that accompanied the pandemic of 2020. The gratifying discovery for many leaders was that so many employees were amazingly resilient. They united around common purposes to serve their customers, employees, and communities; improvised new work schedules; learned to reach beyond habits of professional distance; and supported colleagues facing tough challenges (such as single parents). Many found relief from the stress by helping neighbors or even strangers impacted by physical, emotional, or financial stress.

Even in industries decimated by long-term shutdowns, such as hospitality (hotels, restaurants, associated travel), we saw a spirit of resilience. Deloitte reported that around the world, "[they help] out our society where they can, for example by making their venue available for hospital beds and hospital employees."[12]

Such extraordinary times show the ingredients for psychological well-being at work. The most basic is the sense of psychological safety that we discussed in Chapters 2 and 6. Next comes a feeling of autonomy, which is the ability to control how one does a job (the opposite of being micromanaged). That contributes significantly to feeling positive about work.[13] Other contributors to psychological well-being are feelings of belonging, of serving a purpose, and of personal efficacy. Hotel employees who put on protective gear and hosted healthcare workers during the pandemic were serving a higher cause than a paycheck. Working as a team, they made a difference in those healthcare workers' lives and, by extension, the lives of their patients.

At the high end of psychological well-being at work is the ability to reach out beyond oneself for the benefit of others. Offering friendship is an outward expression, as are giving and receiving gratitude from colleagues. The gestures do not have to be heroic; simple interest and consideration is a fine place to start. Dr. Dacher Keltner suggested to us this simple advice: "Go out into the world, be clear about your intentions, but also just listen. If you orient toward that simple task, you're going to be okay."

It's hard to achieve psychological well-being in a hostile work environment, but as the pandemic showed, a culture that puts well-being first can thrive even in a hostile physical or economic environment. That's the underlying reason Trusted Teams put well-being at the top of the priority list—it makes the other positive outcomes possible.

Many of the habits and routines we've listed above to promote physical well-being also promote psychological health, in particular healthy sleep, meditation, and exercise. In addition, you can add these activities to your toolbox:[14]

- Stay connected to colleagues, friends, and family. One of the best substitutes for "How are you doing?" is "How can I support you?" (but don't overcommit yourself).
- Do the same with your professional network. Whether through email or sites like LinkedIn, maintaining a larger network of people doing similar work and facing similar challenges benefits your psychological well-being as well as your career.
- Get creative about coping mechanisms. When social distancing restrictions meant Jen couldn't get to the gym, she invented a "driveway workout" that was great exercise and also got a friendly following on social media.
- Establish boundaries around your time and privacy. When your work life is all give, always saying yes, the opportunities increase for people to deliberately or inadvertently take too much of your time and energy. Group boundaries like "no-email weekends" or "quiet afternoons" create psychological space for concentrated work or rest and recovery.
- Recognize when you need help, and act on it. If stress or overwork is harming your psychological well-being, it's your right and your responsibility to take action. That might mean a difficult discussion with a colleague, accessing an employee assistance program, or talking to a doctor or therapist.
- Practice whatever feeds your positivity, whether that's practicing gratitude/affirmation/journaling daily, learning a new skill, or joining your colleagues to celebrate (in person or virtually) an accomplishment, milestone, or other victory.

Don't Forget Social Well-Being

In its simplest form, social well-being means human connection. The Harvard Study of Adult Development established the importance of good relationships to physical health, mental health, and longevity. At work, social well-being is a huge contributor to the productivity we discussed in regard to Trusted Teams. The connection to others is for many people a big part of why they go to work in the morning.

Social well-being isn't confined to the immediate team, however, and even transactional relationships can contribute to human connections. In a large organization, employees have transactional relationships with many others—people in distant departments they might talk to once a year, but whom they trust based on their common affiliation to the organization. A healthy culture creates a default sense of trust among employees.

For example, you might experience a problem with your network connection. You call the help desk. Someone there creates a ticket, and the problem gets fixed. Maybe you get an email asking if the problem was fixed in a timely manner. These are all transactions, hardly relationships at all, but when they are positive, they contribute in small ways to a sense of trust, connection, and confidence in the group—in short, a sense of social well-being.

To understand the importance of social well-being at work, simply imagine the opposite: an environment where you can't get help, can't get answers, can't trust colleagues to be accountable, can't trust what you are told. Low trust creates high frustration and stress. And if people in the "society" of work are causing that, social well-being suffers.

But when social well-being is part of a culture, people can bring their full human selves to work, and as we'll see, that is central to business success in the modern economy.

KEY POINTS

- Well-being is bigger than physical wellness, and it comes from a diverse set of programs and behaviors that have a positive impact on employees' physical, mental, financial health, and a sense of purpose.
- Workism and a scarcity mindset, grounded in traditional bureaucratic cultures, are the most common threats to well-being in an organization.
- Individual well-being begins with a personal plan; small steps lead to big changes.
- Psychological well-being at work goes beyond safety to include autonomy, a sense of purpose, compassion, and kindness.

CHAPTER 8

MINDS AND HEARTS, WORKING TOGETHER

Our emotions have evolved to help us in two ways:
to communicate with other people, and just as
importantly, to communicate with ourselves.

—Susan David, author of *Emotional Agility: Get Unstuck,
Embrace Change, and Thrive in Work and Life.*[1]

Human skills are the skills of the future. Learning them and using them at work will make you a more valuable employee. Developing your most human skills makes you a more effective player, more open to learning and more able to deal with the realities of today's work: volatility, uncertainty, change, and ambiguity. When teams ground their interactions in human skills, they work better together.

But what exactly are human skills? As computing and artificial intelligence imitate human actions, and go far beyond human abilities to process raw information in some ways, psychologists and other experts describe a landscape of skills that blend human cognition with creativity, intuition, empathy, authenticity, communication, curiosity, psychological resilience, meaning, and even compassion and love. In other words, human skills mean our emotions and intelligence work together to produce better outcomes than either could independently accomplish.

In Chapter 1 we examined how the changing work environment puts a premium on these skills. When researchers survey job descriptions, social skills are second only to complex problem-solving skills in terms of demand. When the World Economic Forum categorized work skills into seven broad categories, 44 percent of the skills needed in workplaces were social skills like coordination with others, emotional intelligence, negotiation, persuasion, and training.[2]

The centrality of human skills to leadership can't be overstated. Take storytelling, for example: Great leaders know that the ability to explain how and why they choose a strategy is an essential skill to any undertaking, from creating a product line to winning a political campaign. Even a business plan crammed with data and research is essentially telling a story about recognizing a need and proposing how to meet it.

As the pace of change increases, the great challenge facing business shifts from managing acute, occasional crises like the financial collapse of 2009 and the COVID-19 pandemic to managing chronic disruption and nonstop change. Organizations facing change need robust social systems to persevere, and social systems are inherently about human interaction—another reason that human skills are the skills of the future.

The small social system we call a Trusted Team therefore must empower its members to focus on humans first and systems second. When faced with chronic disruption, a Trusted Team understands that human skills are what makes strategic change possible.

Social interactions are among the most sophisticated uses of our human skills. Speaking or listening to someone else, we assign meaning to words, facial expressions, physical gestures, attire, pacing, and a dozen other actions involving cultural etiquette (such as pausing to listen versus interrupting or showing respect instead of "mansplaining"). Magnify those conscious and unconscious meanings with status, power, respect, disrespect, trust, and mistrust, and you can see that even a simple team meeting is a symphony of applied human skills.

Strengthening your human skills at work begins with understanding your own mindset and how your intelligence and emotions work together to direct what you do. Grounded in self-knowledge, you then expand the radius of your understanding to how you present yourself and how you are perceived. As you develop critical skills like empathy and emotional intelligence, you also develop the courage and confidence to bring human skills to the front of interactions (instead of burying them under a misguided "professional" persona). The result is a culture of well-being among team members, as opposed to privately residing within each person.

Mindset and Emotions

Psychologist Carol Dweck's groundbreaking work established that mindset is a powerful determinant of a person's ability to achieve full potential. To simplify her concept: People with a "fixed" mindset believe that ability (or intelligence or performance) is static and unchanging through life. They attribute failure to insufficient ability. As a result, they tend to avoid challenges, ignore useful negative feedback, surrender to strong obstacles, feel threatened by the success of others, and see effort as having a limited effect on outcomes in work. People with a "growth" mindset believe ability (and thus performance) can be developed and improved. They attribute failure to insufficient effort or the wrong approach. As a result, they embrace challenges, learn from negative feedback, persist against setbacks or obstacles, find lessons and energy regarding others' success, and see effort as the path to success.[3]

Mindset has strong implications for personal growth. Looking at a personal challenge, such as improving one's health or a particular work skill, the fixed mindset tends to focus on limitations and the growth mindset sees possibilities:

> "I'm just not a good listener," says the fixed mindset.
>
> "I can learn to listen to my team members more carefully," says the growth mindset.

The fixed mindset isn't necessarily lazy, but its focus on limitations is a subconscious brake on progress. A person with a fixed mindset might try a new diet or a new work habit, but when success is slow, that person tends to return to familiar and safe routine. In contrast, a person with a growth mindset might try a new diet or work habit and respond to slow progress with persistent effort. The growth mindset seeks feedback and adjusts behavior in search of success.

When we discuss bringing your human self to work, we ask people to adopt a growth mindset—to be persistent in the face of adversity. Overcoming adversity calls for emotional strength and adaptiveness to change. It requires us to face our thoughts and feelings, use them as feedback, and move ahead.

Unfortunately, a common belief in many organizations is that emotions don't belong in the workplace. That's a logical fallacy—one of our defining characteristics as humans is a complex emotional life. As the University of Southern California neuroscientist Antonio Damasio has said, humans aren't thinking machines, "but rather feeling machines that think."[4] Bringing our whole selves to work means accepting, not avoiding, our emotions.

To thrive in this uncertain world, we could all use a little more "emotional agility"—a term used by psychologist Dr. Susan David (and the title of her book). She says, "Our emotions indicate our needs, and they have evolved to help us in two primary ways. First, they help us to communicate with other people, to ask for help, to get support, or to let people know what our needs are. Second, they help us communicate with ourselves. So often, we feel tough emotions when things are butting up against our values or when we feel a sense of dissonance or when we are not being seen. This dual communicative purpose is true today in our organizations, in how we love and live and come to our relationships. We can use awareness of our emotions to calibrate ourselves and to bring ourselves forward most effectively."

She continues: "One of the largest misunderstandings of emotions is that 'good' emotions are all about joy and happiness and 'bad' emotions are about anxiety and frustration, and thus we should push those 'bad' emotions aside. When we call some emotions bad, that's associated with lower levels of well-being, high levels of mental distress, and a feeling of being stuck. . . . The capacity to be capacious and courageous enough to go toward those difficult emotions is often what brings us to better ways of being in the world."[5]

A growth mindset looks at emotions like anxiety and frustration and accepts them as valuable cues that something needs attention. Rather than pushing them aside or condemning them, or seeing oneself as deficient or weak for experiencing those emotions, a growth mindset asks, "What in this situation, or in myself, is causing these feelings?"

Remember the last time you experienced a conflict at work. It could be the result of having a difference of opinion, having differing ideas about a way forward on a project, witnessing unacceptable behavior, or just being in a meeting with someone who rubs you the wrong way. Maybe you were interrupted in a meeting. Maybe you encountered a frustrating delay and had to explain this to your boss. Ask yourself how you felt at the time. You might remember an emotion like frustration because a situation was out of your control, but you would have to face the consequences. You might feel physically tense, remembering that aggressive team member who talked over you or ignored your suggestions.

Now think of the emotion you felt as a messenger (you might be feeling it again as you read this). What is it telling you? What thoughts and mental screenplays does it trigger? If the feeling is anger, do you imagine telling someone off, correcting the person, shutting him or her down, or even getting revenge? None of those brief imaginings are real, they aren't yet facts, but they feel real to your emotional mind. Sometimes we might spend minutes, hours, days, or even years rehashing the original offense as the beginning of a whole imaginary story about "what happened to me and what I did about it."

The moment you see the emotion and the reaction it triggers, however, is also the moment you can step to one side mentally and ask, "What is this emotion telling me?" If anger, it might be telling you that someone's behavior is unacceptable. If frustration, it might be telling you that your plans for the project to go well, and all the good feelings you experience in a success, were snatched away from you. Suddenly you can't have what you had imagined would be yours. You have to recalibrate your day and your emotional state.

Taking that moment to distance ourselves just a bit from our emotions, without denying they exist, is the beginning of emotional agility. As Susan David describes the experience, "It's about noticing your thoughts, your emotions and stories for what they are. They are thoughts; they are emotions; they are stories; they are not fact. Then you can ask yourself, who do I want to be in this moment, what are my values that I can bring forward so that I'm not hooked by this difficult experience. With a growth mindset, difficult emotions can be an opportunity to be healthy with ourselves. We don't have to deny our feelings, but we can consciously choose to move ahead in the direction of our values and how we bring ourselves into the world."

In a team setting at work, this attention to our emotions empowers us to move through conflict (or, for that matter, success) in the direction of shared values. In the context of Trusted Teams, being mindful of how we are feeling, and nonreactive to the immediate moment, empowers us to bring healthy relationships and well-being into the flow of work.

"You Have to Be Vulnerable"

Our colleague Tatiana Dominguez, in the Office of the Chief Technology Officer, described the balancing acts that bringing the human self to work requires of leaders:

> The first consideration with having relationships at work, especially if they are reporting relationships, is that you have to be vulnerable. In a leadership role, you do need to be mindful of your degree of vulnerability so as not to erode confidence in your ability to lead and move the team forward. For me, it's how I bring my authentic self to work and allows for team member(s) to be vulnerable, too. It results in rich dialog, deep connections, and a positive work environment.
>
> The second consideration is caring for people deeply while being honest and direct with them. When people know that you genuinely care about them (and their families and their development), your bond makes it much easier to give them feedback, especially tough feedback. I like to offer personal examples of mistakes I've made and how I've corrected course in the past (again calling on vulnerability as a way of relating to my team). My family knows the people on my team. In fact, my circle of

coworkers has always been an extended family. I have numerous friendships that have lasted from previous jobs and companies.

Bonds at work are important because those colleagues may be the only ones (more than family or friends outside of work) that know what challenges you're facing and the context in which you're facing them. You need to hear advice that you can't give yourself. It's important to have people who are in the same boat with you, who can put a mirror in front of you for you. Nurturing those relationships takes time and dedication. I keep regularly scheduled calls with colleagues inside and outside of my organization and focus on relationships that fill my cup and leave me energized and empowered and ensure that I can provide the same to them. We all can use more cheerleaders!

What You Project

Long-term trust among team members depends on authenticity. Showing up as our most genuine selves allows our energy to be directed toward accomplishing work instead of that energy being diverted into saving face or gaining advantage. If that's the case, why is it so hard for many of us to feel we are fully authentic at work?

The workism we described earlier is a major factor driving ourselves away from authentic human interaction. We've looked at how workist attitudes damage our individual health; they also direct our professional personas away from our authentic selves.

Psychologist Carl Jung defined "persona" as the personality or self that we project to others, a behavioral mask that is somewhat different from who we know ourselves to be. It's a powerful concept—that "All the world's a stage/And all the men and women merely players," as Shakespeare wrote—and uncounted books are devoted to the phenomena of personas. For the purpose of building well-being into our teams and ourselves, we'll limit our discussion to the effect of inauthentic personas at work.

We navigate work relationships using professional personas, and they are essential to social functioning. Without conforming to expected behaviors, people are basically governed by their impulses, like children. Expected behaviors are like the shared basic assumptions of a company's culture, and they exist for the same reason—to facilitate social functioning in order to get work done. Professional personas can be understood as a framework that supports those interactions.

For example, if a leader projects a professional persona that tolerates mistakes in others with calm and reason, colleagues can take risks at work without fear of being on the receiving end of anger, intolerance, or unfair criticism. Conversely, if someone rages at mistakes, colleagues learn not to take risks or will cover up errors as a matter of psychological and professional survival.

The trouble in teams arises when the created persona is incompatible with the authentic person. If a person says, "All mistakes are learning experiences," but secretly believes people who make an error are incompetent, that person's interactions are inauthentic. The inauthentic persona prevents the mistake from being a learning experience after all.

If we see ourselves as accountable, we might assume others agree. But if we frequently take on deadlines we can't hit, and then apologize or make excuses, people will react to our persona with mistrust.

Even in a "positive" interaction, a false persona can subvert teamwork. If someone's persona is relentlessly positive, that person might avoid healthy disagreements. The desire to avoid conflict prevents progress that could otherwise happen when differences are resolved openly.

It takes courage to present an authentic persona, because a false persona is psychological armor against conflict or error. Taking off that armor means risking a hit to the "real me" instead of the "work me." When we take off our psychological armor at work, we need the resilience of a growth mindset and emotional agility. Then we can come to work as our genuine selves and direct our energy toward the values and actions we believe in. Even though the risk of personal authenticity can be high, the rewards—integrity, transparency, and courage—are worth it.

To let go of our armor, to be our genuine selves, is not easy even in the healthiest workplaces. We acquire our psychological defenses from an early age. We don't automatically become emotionally agile and authentic and bring our values to work once we decide they're worthwhile, but if we rally around human values in our teams, including the acceptance that we are going to make mistakes and to start and stop and progress slowly, we will make progress as individuals and as teams.

What Others Perceive

Understanding how we are perceived by others is a mirror that reflects our personas and our choice of whether or not we act authentically. Since others are probably wearing their psychological armor, too, this can only be achieved through clear communication. So many problems are caused because we unconsciously assume others see us as we see ourselves.

The trouble caused by a disconnect between a person's persona and behavior might be addressed by friends or colleagues at work, but if not, it's up to leaders or mentors to point out the problem to an individual and work with the person to remedy it. Mistaken attribution is a special danger here—you don't necessarily know the cause of a problem unless you hold a candid conversation that is clear on the problem but easy on the person. Nothing makes someone add another layer of psychological armor like being misunderstood.

People at the far end of the introverted scale are often misunderstood.[6] One of us knows an entrepreneur who is intensely quiet. He gives a lot of one-word answers to questions, and conversations are sometimes filled with long pauses. The extroverts dealing with him have to keep reminding themselves that he's not annoyed, or angry, or bored. He's just being his authentic self. It's not his intention or his responsibility that, because of their garrulous nature, extroverts on his team react with discomfort— it's their responsibility to communicate well and understand he's simply presenting an authentic persona very different from theirs.

A growth mindset can appreciate a diverse variety of temperaments and personas on a team.

When the people on Anh's team adopt their stance of Radical Candor with each other, misunderstandings don't lead to a spiral of personal conflict. For instance, someone might note that it's taking longer to complete a section of research in the time allotted. The person waiting for that research in order to continue with his or her part of the project doesn't jump to a reflexive response of "Now you've messed up the schedule," but instead responds collaboratively, saying, for example, "I hear you're having trouble. How can we solve this together? How do we make sure the whole project stays on track?"

This attitude of challenging the implicit assumptions (the schedule) while acting with care toward the person can reach through the person's psychological armor. Even if there are hidden reasons why the armor stays on (such as a difficulty in someone's personal life), the focus on solving the problem rather than changing the person enables the group to keep functioning well.

"We're Best Friends to This Day"

Creating strong relationships doesn't have to be complicated. Sometimes it's enough to blow off the stress together, says our colleague Natalie Martella:

> For three years, I traveled from my home in Pennsylvania to a project in Oregon, sometimes spending only two days a week with my family. But the friendships we created among the team gave us all support. The team would have dinners together in furnished apartments, and one of my teammates would cook us all his grandmother's old Indian dishes, which were amazing. We're best friends to this day.
>
> We also had fun. One member was obsessed with fancy and funny socks, so when I left for another project, I made socks for everyone with all our faces. Another time, a team member with a mustache was leaving and we held a big luncheon, and everyone showed up with stick-on mustaches in honor of him, including the waiter. Simple moments of fun like this really stick with you.

Unintended Perceptions

Our workweeks are minefields of misappropriation simply because of the human tendency to categorize one another, but Radical Candor doesn't require radical changes in behavior. Small steps work.

Imagine a team member named Hector. He's an introverted Guardian who loves to do intense research but is never the most gregarious person in the group. He sits quietly in meetings and answers substantive questions thoroughly but stays silent during casual conversations. He joins a team for an extended assignment, and soon a more outgoing member of the team (Molly) gets the impression he's bored or doesn't want to socialize because he's temporary or thinks he doesn't belong. But that's not Hector's perception or intent—he experiences the group meetings as necessary exchanges, but interaction (especially in groups) takes a lot of energy, and he relishes the chance to get back to research.

Hector doesn't have to become gregarious, but it is helpful for him to understand that the message others perceive in his silence isn't the one he intends. Likewise, Molly's perception that he doesn't want to be there is incorrect; he's just reacting to the extra energy demand that socializing puts on him—the opposite of her experience, which is that interaction is energizing.

The small-step solution to these and other misapprehensions is to become mindful that most interactions are both between people and within individuals, and to show that understanding in simple ways. Hector can ask about somebody's weekend or hobby and then really listen. Molly can understand that her discomfort with Hector's silence has more to do with her lack of identification with being in the world that way. He's not judging her or others; he's just experiencing the same meeting differently from her.

Finding out how you are perceived can also be a path to growth because sometimes our personas are so strong, they prevent us from knowing ourselves. Wharton professor Adam Grant suggested a method for piercing our own armor when he wrote: "Ask people for feedback, and they sometimes tell you what you want to hear. Ask them about blind spots, and they're more likely to tell you what you need to hear. Gains in self-awareness often begin with the question: What do other people know about me that I might not realize?"[7]

It's good advice, so we've learned to prompt our awareness by asking simple questions like, "Am I missing something in this?" and "I'd welcome a suggestion, especially if someone can find a flaw in my assumptions on this plan."

There is a humbling but necessary principle adjacent to this work of presenting our most authentic personas. We must also make room for others' authentic selves as well.

That's not easy if someone's authentic self is very different from yours. In terms of the Deloitte Business Chemistry types, an Integrator might never choose to adopt the persona of a Driver and vice versa. What enables them to work well together is their shared values and their mutual respect for the fact that different types are going to express those values in different ways.

Small Steps, Big Changes

Jonathan Fields, author of *How to Live a Good Life,* commented in a Deloitte *WorkWell* podcast that many people might be further along toward this goal than they realize: "First, you really need to understand yourself—what matters to you, what fills you up psychologically and what empties you out. Then, you look at the work you're doing and the culture you're in and identify where the conflicts are between what fills you up and what empties you out in what you're doing daily. What most people find is that their work has a fairly high level of alignment, but one or two things are definitely off."

Fixing this, says Fields, needn't be an enormous change: "The further you go into life, with obligations to family or a desire for security, you don't blow that up unless you absolutely have to. The investment you make in yourself is to change what you are doing along those things that are off. . . . Very often you can make small changes, sometimes different from what your job description requires, that give you more fulfillment and a sense of flow. We call that job crafting, and research suggests small shifts like this actually allow you to accelerate your growth in a job."

Thriving on Empathy

In the daily dance of impressions you project and perceive, the key human skill is empathy. It is the two-way bridge that enables people to better understand others and convey their authentic persona to others.

Empathy is the ability to identify and share in the emotions and experiences of others (as opposed to sympathy, which is showing concern for someone's feelings but remaining at a psychological distance). Empathy is the foundation of understanding others, but it requires us to step out of our psychological armor and experience another's internal workings. Empathy is more than the intellectual ability to understand another's point of view; it means imagining how another person experiences the world, and doing that accurately. It means questioning our own assumptions about others, and becoming willing to be curious about how they see things.

Empathy includes stepping into someone's positive emotions as well as painful ones. Innovative products, for example, begin with imagining how people might feel about an experience. "How would people feel if they could learn to love cooking at home?" can be answered with feelings like "accomplished," "self-sufficient," "frugal," "luxurious," or "healthy." Depending on which feelings are product goals, the result might be a meal kit subscription, a series of cooking tutorials on the web, or other products. It begins with empathy—internalizing a sensation and then imagining how to create it in others.

Scope and detail are part of the empathetic imagination. A statement like "Imagine a phone you can carry" results in a cell phone. A statement like "Imagine unlimited computing power in your pocket, along with a camera, digital recorder, calculator, and access to all the world's information" results in a smartphone. A statement like "Imagine all those capabilities built into a person's clothing" results in something not yet invented (but we think it sounds very cool).

The field of design is a great example of empathy at work. Imagine a design team creating a hotel lobby. The design team considers how all the users of that hotel lobby, from the registration clerk to the tired business traveler to the child running out to the pool to the young person waiting at the bar for a blind date to arrive, will interact with that environment. The team imagines how every detail will inspire an emotional reaction in each of those persons, with the goal of giving them a good experience. The team runs scenarios composed of little stories for each of those people. Before the first sketches are made, each person on the team has used empathy to feel what the prospective user of that hotel lobby feels.

Can you imagine the richness of that team's discussions? Can you identify with one of the persons in those little scenarios? If so, you too are exercising your power of empathy in this moment, reading words on a page.

Empathy in a work team enables people to imagine the experience of other team members both intellectually and emotionally, which is why it's the key human skill for working together.

First, it makes work more efficient. Empathy enables you to understand what emotions motivate people's words and actions, so they don't have to explain every component of every idea. For example, if someone says, "This place is too noisy for a client meeting," you may infer that she respects the client's comfort. On the other hand, if she says, "I want to focus on the purpose of the meeting and not on distractions" or "It's hard for me to understand speech in a noisy place," your empathy processes all these bits of knowledge quickly, even unconsciously, and you might respond, "You're right. Let's find a quiet room." Without that instant processing, we might spend five minutes discussing the pros and cons of meeting in a noisy courtyard.

Second, empathy reaffirms a bond. When one person demonstrates understanding to another, he is making an effort on the other's behalf. We are connected by our common concern for each other's success and well-being.

Third, empathy builds trust. When you interpret people's words and actions accurately, you show that you understand them and who they are as human beings. Feeling understood is a foundation of a trusting relationship.

Fourth, empathy magnifies intellectual understanding. When focused outward (to a client, a product user, a business partner), empathy goes beyond data to create a deeper, more nuanced picture of someone.

Common to all the reasons above is that empathy enables us to communicate what we understand about another's experience. Even if we misunderstand someone, the act of checking in—"Here's what I think you're saying/feeling/telling me"—is the step that empathy enables us to take. That's the path to clarity, the light that shines through our professional personas and puts us on common ground as we work together.

People sometimes conflate empathy and compassion, so we'll note that empathy precedes compassion but is not quite the same thing. Empathy allows you to feel what another person is experiencing, and compassion is taking the extra step to serve another person's interest.[8] We typically talk of compassion as alleviating someone's need. That can be as simple as answering a question or as profound as joining someone in mourning.

There is a place for compassion at work because it increases organizational well-being. Because compassion moves you to alleviate someone's needs, it inspires kindness in one person and gratitude in another. Well-being rises for both the receiver and the giver, as they take off the armor that alienates organizational life and build a more positive relationship—the key element that makes Trusted Teams so strong.

Empathy in the Time of COVID-19

Humans are social animals, and most of us do not respond well to prolonged isolation. In such a situation, our social skills can become rusty, and we may lose our ability to read social cues. Journalist Kate Murphy cited research on hermits, prisoners, and polar explorers and noted in the *New York Times*: "You get a sidelong glance and immediately think the other person dislikes you. A confusing comment is interpreted as an insult. At the same time you feel more self-conscious, fearing any missteps will put you further at risk."[9]

One paradox of the pandemic was that all the social isolation we experienced caused our teams to come together more closely. Even though social distancing closed our offices, the ways in which we improvised work "alone together" kept our social interactions going, and because there was less chance of spontaneous social interaction, both of us built it into our meetings, beginning them with informal check-ins and sometimes scheduling side conversations just to talk about new activities or ways we were coping with isolation. Short words of commiseration and empathy with team members went a long way to keeping us focused both on work and on the things that matter most to well-being like health, relationships, and a sense of balance. (We'll say more about this in Chapter 9.)

The Well Organization

Prepared with self-awareness and an awareness of how you present yourself and how you are perceived, you can look clearly at your teams and organizations. You're ready to take the next step: applying your human skills to every corner of the workplace.

That doesn't mean every Guardian has to be a social butterfly, or every Pioneer has to bend into being detail oriented. Human skills are as richly diverse as temperaments. It means you have to figure out ways to create moments of connection and teamwork that make the most of everyone's unique emotional and cognitive makeup. You do have to step out of the armor and give attention to human interactions.

This is a time when small steps lead to big changes. You can start by sharing some of your own ideas for well-being with a trusted colleague or two. Some simple examples:

- If you start a habit of taking a lunchtime walk twice a week, ask someone to join you (inviting someone from outside your immediate team is a low-key way to network).
- Tell your team that you want to check email just three times a day and to expect replies then. If there's an emergency, people can call you.
- An idea from Brené Brown: begin each meeting (or teleconference) with participants giving two-word descriptors about how they're feeling. Not "I'm fine," but more authentic statements, such as "I'm excited and grateful" or "I'm interested but worried."[10]
- Ask sincerely how team members are doing with questions like "What's your day been like so far?"

See https://www.linkedin.com/pulse/why-we-need-stop-saying -how-you-jen-fisher for 20 more questions to ask.

The "projected persona versus perceived persona" disconnect is most vivid when a team member acts out a "Do as I say, not as I do" attitude. You could encourage people in your group to find balance, but if you're sending emails at 10 p.m., that's sending the opposite message, especially if you're a team leader or executive. Leaders can get caught up in the fallacy that they have to work harder and later than anyone else, either to justify their power or to defend their position, but that actually sends a contradictory message. From one point of view, employees will think,

"Well, all that talk about balance is just message, not reality." From another point of view, a junior person will witness that behavior and think, "Balance might be for others, but if I want to advance, this is how to do it." At its worst—and this is far too common in organizations—people will internalize the message that they have to respond, have to embrace the imbalanced work life, because big brother/big sister is watching.

The way to prevent these mixed messages is simply to communicate the reasons for behavior in advance. For example, a person might devote several hours to childcare in the afternoon and catch up with work in the evening. Or some people might be at their most productive into the night, and clearly state that they don't expect everyone to have the same preferences. Transparency prevents misunderstanding and exposes potential difficulties (like scheduling) so they can be worked out.

Finally, bringing our human selves to work means confronting our fear of messing up. The need to ignore mistakes, to cover up and save face and rationalize our behavior, is a natural human tendency. It's also a common feature of organizational cultures that reward success and punish failure in a hundred subtle and obvious ways. And if you, like us, have that natural tendency, there's a powerful human habit to adopt: rapid accountability for your own mistakes.

When it comes to relationships, time and technology have a way of magnifying mistakes. The longer you let a mistake go unacknowledged, the worse it tends to feel. The more you hide behind the emotional wall of email, writing long explanations for simple errors, the greater your chance of being misunderstood or mistrusted.

A friend tells this story:

> It was a lousy day. Everything seemed to go wrong at once, and I was feeling harassed and sorry for myself and annoyed

at the world. Walking down the hall about 2 p.m., I saw a table full of sandwiches left over from a meeting, and I grabbed one. A guy I didn't know came out of the nearby conference room and said, "Hey, those are our sandwiches; leave them alone."

I just lost it. I put down the sandwich and sputtered, "Dammit, I didn't know your meeting was going on, and I haven't had lunch, and these are all leftovers, and I just wanted this stupid ham and cheese . . . ," and I stomped off with my mind full of poison for this guy I didn't even know. I had the whole inner monologue going—"Clown won't share food. . . . We all work for the same company. . . . This day can't get worse . . ."

And something stopped me. Something told me to turn around and go back. I walked to him with my hand out and said, "Hey, I'm sorry. I'm just a jerk having a lousy day, and I was out of line there, and I apologize."

He was so surprised! He said, "That's okay; take what you like. And what's your name?" And he introduced himself, and every time we ran into one another after that, we'd chat. All it took was a moment of accountability—a simple admission that I was out of line—and the whole problem went away.

It's a momentary interaction like this that builds up or tears down relationships at work. Accountability can be contagious.

Every time you advocate for your own needs in a way that is professional, kind, and authentic, you are giving others the opportunity to do the same. There's a virtuous cycle of self-awareness that creates more chances to drive the business forward together. If you protect your own well-being, you give people permission to protect theirs.

KEY POINTS

- Blending human cognition with human emotion creates the skills of the future.
- A growth mindset enables us to become aware of our emotional messages and choose how to act.
- Strong relationships are built on understanding what persona you project, and what others perceive.
- Empathy and accountability lead to mutual trust among team members.

CHAPTER 9

OVERCOMING TECHNOLOGY OVERLOAD

There are only two industries that call their customers "users": illegal drugs and software.

—Edward Tufte, Professor Emeritus in Political Science, Computer Science & Statistics, Yale University[1]

We are quick to adopt technology, but slow to adapt to it—and the gap is causing real harm to our bodies, minds, relationships, and organizations.

The first waves of work technology automated and streamlined tasks—the typewriter replaced the pen, and the word processer replaced the typewriter. The telephone and fax machine replaced many business letters, and email and texting replaced many phone calls. The calculator replaced handwritten math, and then the spreadsheet replaced the calculator. Each wave did what the previous technology could do and added new capabilities. Such advances came over years, and they were initially very costly, which slowed their adoption.

As the cost of technology decreased and the usability increased, so did our speed of adoption. Technology has become embedded in our lives much faster than anything else in human history. That includes familiar work technologies like email and office applications and almost invisible information technologies like the specialized chips that monitor and regulate auto emissions, silently sending and receiving data as we drive. As for the speed of technology entering our lives, consider that it took 120 years for US landline telephone subscription ownership to reach 68 per 100 people (in 2000), while mobile phone subscriptions reached that number in 20 years (in 2005). Today, there are 120 cell subscriptions for every 100 Americans.[2]

Social media in particular exploded in use in this century, and the speed with which we adopted social media made it impossible to discover its unhealthy downstream effects before it spread throughout our work lives and personal lives. The benefits of our shiny new tech were instantly apparent, but the cost of using it in the way we do is just recently coming to light.

Now our headlong rush to adopt technology is entering the science fiction realm as the line blurs between people and their technology. The concept has been with us for a while. Researchers Manfred E. Clynes and Nathan S. Kline proposed the term "cyborg" in 1960,[3] and it caught on in the popular imagination to mean a living being that is part human and part robot. More recently, physicist Alan Lightman called such a phenomenon "Homo techno," defining it as "a hybrid of living animal and machine, a heart and soul fused to a computer chip."[4] Lightman used the example of his young grandchild, living half a world away, barely distinguishing Lightman's image on a screen from the flesh-and-blood person.

We're not quite at the point where human brains and computers are fully merged, but our feelings, motivations, and sensory-cognitive feedback mechanisms are already deeply entwined with our technology. Social media is carefully designed to provoke, monitor, and magnify human emotions. It's designed to learn the preferences and reactions of individual people, so each person's experience feels individually tailored. Every upgrade of social media platforms further blurs the sense of separation that people feel between themselves and their devices; in particular, the human act of communicating with other humans feels personal, even intimate, on Facebook, Twitter, Instagram, and the rest.

Starting about 10 years ago, work technology began to blend with social media and mobile computing. Collaboration, timelines, the cloud, and smartphones don't just improve the speed of previous technologies; they are designed to direct how our brains interact with information.[5] They even change our emotional relationship with our work technologies.

But our management thinking and our work relationships have not adapted to the qualitative changes in the way we work, and old ways of thinking about technology are inadequate to this moment. Unless we adapt our behavior to acknowledge this new relationship and make conscious choices about how we use it, both human relationships and well-being will suffer.

Every innovation has unintended consequences (and as we'll see, some intended consequences as well). Arianna Huffington put it well, noting that technology like artificial intelligence and advanced algorithms can have tremendous benefits for our lives, but at the moment they are not making us any more wise or empathetic. In addition, their addictive qualities mean that we need to learn to set boundaries in our relationship with technology.[6] We are beholden to our technology to the extent we simultaneously treasure its benefits and ignore its costs. We need to be deliberate about how we put our technology to work for us versus working for our technology.

Smartphones are owned by almost half the human race,[7] and 2.7 billion people use Facebook monthly.[8] But as business incorporates smartphones and social media into work, we're noticing the cost of this rapid adoption. Technology has no value unless it serves humans, but the same cannot be said in reverse—so the question is, how can we use the best of this latest wave to serve us well and preserve the best of our human qualities?[9]

This chapter is about cyborgs and simulations: it's about the ways in which our very selves have merged with our technology and about the virtual worlds we inhabit. Some of this is a deliberate creation on everyone's part, some of it is unconscious to the user but very much designed into the technology, and some of it has the ominous feeling of addiction, when we know something isn't altogether good for us, but we keep using it anyway.

To think about how we adapt, it helps to understand the design elements adopted from social media. Work technology and social media offer the great benefits of connecting us to an infinite number of people and an unlimited amount of information, but both demand we pay for our usage with our truly finite human resources: time and attention.

The design of social media is based on a "variable reward system," meaning it doles out rewards unpredictably but periodically as you use it. You scroll through your feed on Facebook or Twitter, on Instagram or Pinterest or any of the others, and you are occasionally rewarded with something that triggers a strong reaction in your brain. It might be a picture of your brand-new grandchild or a funny picture of a friend's pet. It might be an intriguing recipe or a fascinating news story. When you encounter that, your brain's pleasure center puts out that little hit of dopamine, and you feel good. Soon the pleasure wears off, and you continue in search of another hit.

It's not just about pleasure. When you see something in your timeline that prompts anger or fear or outrage, you also experience a more excited state of mind. Your brain is activated by what you perceive as bad news or injustice, a threat to you or your "tribe." There goes that little chemical surge. And you respond to that surge by continuing to scroll, in quest of more.

The Tech Casino

It's not accidental that this sounds like turning your phone into a very sophisticated slot machine. Adam Alter, associate professor of marketing and psychology at the NYU Stern School of Business and author of *Irresistible: The Rise of Addictive Technology and the Business of Keeping Us Hooked,* told us that the features in social media sites are based on the psychological insights first used in the 1950s in casinos.

"There are no clocks in casinos," Adam notes. "The version of that in [social media] is an experience in which you have no sense that time is passing. The content that arrives on your screen has been weaponized over time to be maximally addictive, and every little feature has been optimized to extract an extra minute or two of your attention. There are a lot of hooks that are embedded that are designed to get us interested and then to keep us engaged."[10]

The platforms have also eradicated "stopping cues" that would interrupt your engagement. Likes and retweets and emojis and especially visual signals such as pictures and video propel your experience forward without a symbol to pause and move to another activity.

Adam told us that the tools are appearing outside social media, for example, in entertainment services. "Once, streaming video required that you do something to move on to the next piece of content. Now, the default is that the next piece of content starts playing 10 seconds after the previous one ends. The single most effective tool these companies have at their disposal is to help you forget that you are engaging in the moment, because then you're less likely to move on."[11]

Social media companies make money by selling users' attention to advertisers. That's their incentive to increase the amount of time you spend on social media; every design decision is based on increasing your time scrolling and interacting with your screen. We aren't saying social media isn't useful or fun; we are saying that its design is intended to get you habituated (or addicted) to receiving those tiny hits of chemical reward.

Business technology operates along a similar vector—rewarding attention. The problems arise when the design or interaction with business tech becomes as unconsciously addictive and mindless as scrolling through a social media feed. When your relationship to email and collaboration platforms crosses over from useful tool to addictive activity, it's difficult to break away even though your productivity declines (see Chapter 1).

Feel Your Own Programming

How long ago did you check your email?

As you read this book, you will probably feel the periodic urge to check your email, office communication, messages, or social media. Can you feel it now? When do these messages bubble up from your unconscious?

> Should I get to that other task?
>
> Have I been reading too long?
>
> How far to the end of this chapter?
>
> What's happening on Instagram/Facebook/Twitter/Slack/Teams/etc.?
>
> Was that a notification banner I saw on my phone a few minutes ago? Phone call or message?
>
> What am I missing out on?

If you're like us, you can feel that little urge many, many times in a day . . . including while reading this book.

The Price We Pay for Overscrolling

Social media runs on attention and advertising. People run on sleep, food, conversation, passion, purpose, ideas.

But our habituation to technology has an exaggerating effect, and the fact that we can do so much makes us feel like we should be doing everything, all the time. We take our phones to bed and start "doomscrolling" through messages. We check email during a two-minute wait in line at the grocery store.

Mobile technology eradicates the boundary between work and life, and even physical settings don't disturb our underlying feeling of power and obligation to work anywhere, anytime. The good news is, we can work at the beach. The bad news is—we choose to work at the beach. We stand awestruck by a sunset on the sea, and our habituated minds interrupt that serene moment with worries, plans, to-do lists, intentions, and the urge to check the email we checked 30 minutes ago—or an impulse to post that moment on social media rather than just enjoying it.

"The only limitations we have are the ones we give ourselves" used to be an inspiring message to go for the greatest goals we can imagine. Now we need to change our view of limitations: we choose to set boundaries on our own relationship to technology, information, and the unachievable goal of doing it all. We used to think the things that slow us down would limit our capacity to achieve our goals. Now is the time to realize that our conscious choices to slow down, to step away from the information stream, are exactly what we need to achieve our goals.

It's the paradox of our work lives that our abundance of power and information has made the most human gifts, like wisdom and empathy, scarce resources.

As use of digital media has skyrocketed, happiness has declined. Professor Jean M. Twenge of San Diego State University cites numerous studies suggesting that Americans are less happy because they have shifted their nonwork activities from social interaction, exercise, and sleep to interacting with screens.[12]

The physical and mental costs of too much screen time include:

> *Poor sleep.* Blue light from our screens reduces the body's melatonin required for good sleep. Some people believe that taking melatonin at night can compensate, but that's a similar behavior to the stimulant-depressive cycle of too much caffeine and alcohol—in the long run, we're regulating systems as compensation rather than addressing the cause. As mentioned in Chapter 7, poor sleep results in a long list of physical and mental problems.

> *Social costs of physical disconnection.* Substituting face-to-face relationships with screen-to-screen interaction often causes people to ignore those around them, like family and friends. Not only does this substitute an "unnatural," intermediated relationship for face-to-face interaction; it alters our basic social structures. The problem isn't that all technological connection is bad (again, it can bring us "together" over long distances); it's that we're substituting managed technological interaction for one-to-one human interaction. The presence of the phone—its interface, the size of a two-dimensional image, its interruptions with notifications and prompts—alters the social experience.

> *Anxiety, depression, and poor judgment.* Recent research has found that conditions of scarcity impose a kind of "cognitive tax" on individuals.[13] For example, an experiment that involved focusing low-income persons' attention on a scenario in which they urgently needed to raise several thousand dollars resulted in the equivalent of a 13-point drop in IQ. (This is similar to the drop in IQ someone would experience after going a

night without sleep.) The phenomenon has similar effects on overloaded individuals who experience scarcity of time. This raises the concern that digital firehoses of poorly filtered information can hamper our ability to pay attention, make good decisions, and stick to plans. And when we try to compensate for interruptions by working faster, we only get more frustrated and stressed. (Ironically, the opposite technology—content precisely filtered to reinforce our beliefs—leads to confirmation bias and a distorted view of the world.)

Information overload is not only distracting, but potentially mentally damaging. We live with a finite amount of time and a limitless well of information and choices, often resulting in a phenomenon called FOMO (fear of missing out). Before we're done responding to a prompt, our devices alert us to the next opportunity, swamping us with the sense that we are not accomplishing an activity we momentarily engaged in.[14]

Social media present us with a world of people more beautiful, accomplished, famous, rich, healthy, what-have-you than ourselves while also prompting us to project the same image. We don't know who we are online. This conflict engenders emotions like contempt and dislike for ourselves, as well as negative judgment. As a result, we live in a kind of fictional world in which we are at once powerful and insufficient.

That fictional world can become sinister, as when social media is weaponized to divide people. It enables participants to inspire emotions such as shock, fear, indignation, and outrage without controls on the veracity of their claims. Nonstop scrolling results in information overload and subsequent feelings of powerlessness. The shallowness of social media interactions weakens social ties, trust, and feelings of autonomy. Social media's design goal—to get you to keep scrolling—means it's specifically engineered to prevent long, thoughtful pauses during which you consider what another person has said or done and your response. Feel angry? Hit back and hit "Send"!

One of the world's leading experts on positive psychology is Amy Blankson. She suggested in a Deloitte *Work Well* podcast that actual "addiction" to social media might only apply to a small percentage of the general population. She prefers a term like "propensity" or "weakness," which bypasses the question of medical definitions—and asks us to consider our relationship to tech in less dire terms. "Technology is neither good nor bad," she says, "But it is a magnifier of things that are already going on in your life. So if you have a propensity to overwork, then technology may exacerbate that. If you have a desire to spend time on games online, technology will now enable you to do those longer."[15]

For the great majority of people who are overusing technology but haven't yet slipped into a medically defined addiction, the good news is that they can enjoy the benefits of digital tools without destroying their relationships or well-being. Becoming conscious of the role that tech plays in your life, and choosing wisely when to pick up the phone and when to put it down, is the first step.

Living Well with Technology

Since the problem with social media and work technologies is that they draw you into mindless participation, the first step in regulating their impact on your life is to become aware of all the moments you feel the impulse to jump back into the timeline or newsfeed or email in-box. Call it awareness, self-knowledge, or mindfulness—the goal is the same: to make deliberate rather than unconscious choices about what to do with your time.

Mindfulness is associated with the practice of meditation, but we learned a distinction between them from a conversation with

Emiliya Zhivotovskaya. As noted earlier in the book, she's a positive psychologist and CEO of The Flourishing Center; and in a Deloitte *WorkWell* podcast she offered this clarification:

> Mindfulness is a way of being in the world, and meditation is a practice that supports that. There are people who choose to meditate from a spiritual perspective [but] there are forms of meditation that I think of as very basic brain training. We have an emotional response within our brain that's usually coming from what we call our core brain or our limbic system, and then we have our rational human part of our brain which is our neocortex.
>
> So, for example, let's say I am at the gym and I have this little compulsion with me: it is like, I wonder if I got an email; I should check my phone. So every time I give into that impulse, I am giving more power to my emotional brain and taking power away from my prefrontal cortex, the part of my brain that is like the controller. So I am not going to think of that moment as a meditation moment, but it is a mindfulness moment; it's me catching myself acting compulsively, and saying "I don't need to check my phone right now. I can finish my workout and my email will wait."[16]

When engaging with technology, that pause of momentary awareness enables you to make a conscious choice about what you will do with your time; it's a way of inserting your own stopping cues. You answer the little compulsion to check your phone by simply recognizing what's going on and talking back to that compulsion—"The email will wait."

Cultivating self-awareness, whether you call it mindfulness or just noticing, isn't a matter of sternly imposing your will on an impulse. It's a matter of creating microhabits throughout your day that interrupt the flow of compulsive or habitual work.

In *The Power of Habit*, reporter Charles Duhigg expertly described the three-part cycle of habitual behavior: there's a cue (you look at your phone on the desk); which triggers a routine (you pick up the phone, unlock it, press the email app); and a reward (there's an update at work or a new email from a friend). The key to changing a habit is to introduce new routines and rewards when the cue hits—in effect substituting a better habit for the old one.[17]

As we've noted throughout this book, we advocate making big changes by taking small steps that interrupt the mindless or habitual flow of our daily lives. Little behaviors can shift your attention out of the trance of habit (as mindfulness teacher Tara Brach calls it) and direct you to make choices.

For example, we know that multitasking doesn't exist on a conscious level. What we call multitasking is actually shifting conscious attention from one task to another.[18] Because multitasking diminishes performance, it's a great opportunity for a change of habit. Substituting simple "monotasking" cues can do that; for example:

- Open only one window per screen on your computer, or one application, at a time. Deal with email and then close it to work on a document.
- Manage the notifications on your computer and your phone more intentionally, so that you are only being interrupted or notified for information that is urgent.
- Similarly, try a "just one thing" rule. Begin with a 15-minutes block of time to focus on one task. If you become distracted, promise yourself that you can get to another activity when 15 minutes are up. Try this for a week, and the following week expand the time to 20 minutes, then 25, leading to the next trick.

- Set aside 30-minute blocks of time for focused work. One microhabit that works for teams is to block out uninterruptable time on the calendar. (Jen's team does this for dedicated growth activities—"Learning Friday" has two hours on the calendar dedicated to learning new skills or information related to work.)
- Put your phone on airplane mode for those 30 minutes. Or as Amy Blankson suggests, simply hide your phone at predetermined times.
- Leave room for surprises: block 30 minutes late in the workday to deal with matters urgent enough to need your attention the same day.
- If you use your phone to check the time, substitute a watch and put the phone away while concentrating. Just eliminating the visual cue of seeing your phone can cut the number of times the urge to check social media or news strikes.
- When talking on the phone or teleconferencing, turn off/put away all other screens. Allow yourself only paper and pen for note taking.
- For a day, change the lock screen on your phone to a message like, "Is this necessary?" or "Really?" Just this prompt can help you cut back on unconscious, habit-driven use.

You can practice monotasking at home as well. Adam Alter told us he puts his phone away during dinner whether he's with family, colleagues, friends, or alone in a restaurant. "You might spend 30 minutes being just a little bored," he said. "And it's fine for that to happen, because you're developing a habit, going through FOMO for a few minutes, but after you get past that initial withdrawal symptom, it becomes something you really look forward to."[19]

The Digital Detox

Cutting back on multitasking is a strong step toward getting right in your relationship with technology. Self-awareness plus new habits leads to self-care, which is essential for well-being. Up to this point we've talked about adding habits, but when we deal with FOMO or habituated interaction with technology, a little more introspection can be helpful. At Deloitte, we ask people to answer five questions as a lighthearted (but also serious) quiz:

- Am I missing out on work or life activities because I am interacting with technology?
- Is my phone/tablet the first thing I look at when I wake up in the morning?
- Do I feel anxious if I can't use my technology?
- Does my technology use impact my personal relationships?
- Do I feel the need to immediately respond when I receive notifications?

The score for this quiz is simple: if you answer yes to *any* of these, maybe it's time to consider a digital detox.

Our digital detox invites you to take one step a day to study your attachment to digital tech. You can choose one activity each day or accrue the activities sequentially (keep doing Monday's step on Tuesday, Monday's and Tuesday's steps on Wednesday, etc.). The goal isn't to punish yourself or cut the cord forever, but to interrupt the nonstop flow of tech-related activities and habits.

Here's the suggested program:

Monday. Stay off social media for the entire day. Substitute other activities. For example, if you typically scroll through a timeline during a break, substitute 30 minutes of walking (outdoors if possible) while listening to an audiobook or informative podcast. Add a usage app on your phone that will report how much time you spent, and on which apps, on a weekly basis.

Tuesday. Eat all your meals in a room without a TV, phone, computer, or other screen. Bonus points for eating with people who are doing the same, trying a bit of conversation.

Wednesday. Don't look at your phone/tablet/computer until you arrive at work. Don't open work email or apps in the evening. Try the 30-minute focused work-time block above.

Thursday. Unsubscribe from all unwanted emails; unfollow anyone you don't know on social media (*alternative:* if you use social media for news, cut half your follows). In the evening, change your phone display to grayscale for the remainder of the week.

Friday. Move any mobile apps you have not used in the past month to a folder to cut down clutter. Turn off push notifications in your phone's settings.

Saturday. Turn your phone off for eight consecutive hours (when you're awake!). Leave your smartwatch at home and go outside.

Sunday. Create a charging station for all your devices away from the bedroom. When you turn in, leave phones, tablets, watches, etc., charging there. Use an alarm clock or radio to replace your phone's alarm.

Some people find it helpful to enlist a friend or colleague as an accountability partner in a digital detox. If you do, check in once a day to talk about how it's going. In particular, talk to each other about your mental reactions to cutting back on the mindless behaviors like opening a newsfeed every time you switch activities. What does the absence of such habits feel like?

It can also help to keep a diary of the week—what did you try, and how did it go? For example, does switching your phone to grayscale reduce its attractiveness or make you more deliberate about use? Without notifications, do you miss anything really important?

If someone at work notices a difference, such as you taking longer to respond to inquiries on email or office communication apps, you can explain that you're trying to become more focused on the work that matters, more conscious about how you use your time, and more deliberate about technology's role in your day. If the person is a friend, you might explain further that a digital detox is about becoming more mindful about everything you do in your life at work and outside of work.

Because that's exactly what it is.

Bring It to Work

You might be reluctant to try a digital detox when it comes to work because, in addition to your own habituation, you are likely surrounded by others with the same habits—or you feel pressure from a work culture where a timely response to digital communication is expected. You might feel a self-created pressure to actively respond and demonstrate that you are visibly working—a kind of digital "look-busy" anxiety. Maybe the vestiges of workism at your business make it hard to speak up about developing healthier habits. In this case, the first question to ask is, why does it seem hard?

We have all kinds of relationships with family, friends, and colleagues, and we all have varying degrees of trust. You'll find that at the bottom of a nervous feeling about changing habits is a bad experience you've had or witnessed. It could be a mocking comment about well-being practices. It could be a hard-driving culture. It could be either that you don't really want to give up those little shots of adrenalin or that you're caught up in your own self-judgment. A lot of people starting well-being habits experience these and other roadblocks.

One way to get around reluctance is to turn to the most meaningful relationships for support and partnership. You don't have to get up at the all-hands meeting and announce, "I'm starting a digital detox because I think technology is taking too much of my productive time!" See if you can go back to the healthy team relationships we described earlier and simply say, "Let's try this." Microhabits can be started in microgroups.

The members of Anh's team developed their set of Everyday Equations as a team, and they hold each other accountable for observing the priorities and revisiting them periodically. There's no criticism involved in reminding someone about the mutually agreed equations. In a similar way, you can team up with one or two other people who think developing new habits around technology is a good idea for well-being and productivity at the same time. In Anh's group, there is even a rotating informal title called "culture champion," the job of which is to point out when the group strays from its intention. (Groups have a way of falling into habits, even elaborate habitual routines, that are just as mindless as individual habits.)

A lot of people feel powerless to change their organizations. We tell our teams that a feeling of powerlessness doesn't let you off the hook—you're still accountable for either changing a culture that needs changing or sustaining a culture you don't like by going along with it. Regardless of your current workplace culture, we all have some ability to create the culture we want, and the best way to make a change is to set an example. It could be that your determination to evolve from tech-bound cyborg to human being will start a cultural change in your team or your organization. Each individual contributes to and helps shape the team's environment and culture. It's as true for teams as it is for people: small steps lead to big changes.

Even though employees must use companywide technologies to do their jobs, *how* they use them comes with a degree of choice. One of the strangest ways in which people interact is to email or send a message with a question to someone working 20 feet away, when walking over to ask a question, or calling and having a real conversation, would work just as well (or maybe better). Even when we say, "I didn't want to interrupt her," we've created a technological signal—rather than wait to ask the question, we place it in the person's work queue. We can look at that as considerate, or as burdensome, but either way it looks like the instant reaction to an impulse is to turn to the tech rather than the moment of human contact.

We are not Luddites—we use work technologies all day long (especially communication tech in these days of virtual teams). We love it. The question isn't whether someone is pro- or anti-technology. It's whether we are actually willing to separate our cyborg minds from automatic reliance on technology, and choose a more deliberate, relationship-rich way of working.

Email has always posed a special temptation. It is ubiquitous, and we use it all day, but we forget that it's an imperfect communication tool. The sender's intention of respectful brevity can be mistaken for offensive curtness. Or overexplaining on the part of the sender can tax the receiver's patience.

Each member of our teams can tell similar stories, and so we have an informal habit of pausing and asking "How would I feel receiving this?" before we hit the Send button. (Sometimes we use the "read aloud" function in our email, just to slow things down.)

Our colleague Kelly Gaertner gives this advice to her team: "Working in a virtual world leaves for an abundance of interpretation; between many emails, instant-messaging pings, or even how you show up on a teleconference, your words/reactions/actions can be interpreted in many ways. I often remind myself of two things: (1) trust your team; support the members in any way that you can but empower and give them space to get things done in the way that's true to them, and (2) assume good intent, always."

Teams can flip the script on alienating technologies by the choices they make. For example, Anh's team has an MS Teams channel called the Water Cooler, where the team members gather from time to time asynchronously to show pictures of their pets, or talk about the latest films and shows, or show a video of last week's backyard camping "trip" with their children. We note with pleasure that the more junior members of the team are quite happy to connect on a personal level, which is something the more senior members (attached as they are in their "professional" personas) can use as an object lesson.

Living in the Simulation

The COVID-19 pandemic thrust millions into the virtual world of collaboration, meeting, and video tools, which we half-jokingly call simulations. It's a marvel how quickly work teams adapted to new visual cues like grids, and how accepting groups were of the fact that some people will adapt a little less quickly than others.

In addition to learning new ways of working and new technologies, people had to adjust to new support systems that were unevenly distributed. Instead of the common conference room, some people met from cramped, noisy apartments and others from spacious patios. Some people enjoyed the companionship of a spouse or roommates, some enjoyed solitude, and others suffered all the ills of chronic loneliness, with teleconferencing on screens a poor substitute for human contact. (And these were the fortunate people who kept their jobs while millions became unemployed!)

The unwanted business case was upon us: millions were compelled to participate in a massive worldwide experiment in virtual work. People had to learn to be amateurs again, a practice that took patience, empathy, and mentoring less technically adept or comfortable colleagues. Journalist Fareed Zakaria observed about his own team, "When you use any teleconferencing mechanisms, you are spending social capital; you're not building it. . . . There was a lot of frustration and raw nerves and hurt feelings because [we] had lost all those [ways] that you could signal to people that you liked them and you were friendly. . . . All that was gone, and all that was left was the work stuff."[20]

Even after we return to some new version of normal, the pandemic experience of working in the simulation can inspire us to bring a little more empathy to our work. Learning and listening to one another takes effort, and it can raise our awareness of other people's feelings and frustrations, if we are mindful and kind enough to sense their struggles.

American companies increased the total percentage of work-from-home days fourfold during the pandemic (from 5 percent to 20 percent). According to *The Economist*, it seems likely that many firms will adopt a model in which large numbers split their working hours between solitary work at home and collaboration in the office.[21] Virtual teams like ours were established before the pandemic, and their techniques of working well together are becoming more widely accepted.

(While some service jobs like package delivery or jobs in critical retail sectors like grocery or hardware thrived in the pandemic, others like those in the restaurant or hospitality industry did not recover nearly as fast as most high-wage jobs. Many might be permanently lost.)

If virtual teams become more widespread in coming years, there will be huge implications that ripple through the economy. What happens to downtown office districts? To businesses that depend on commuters (transportation, auto dealerships)? What is the long-term effect of not seeing people in person nearly as much as we used to? Will a large part of the workforce feel as isolated as scientists in the Antarctic or the International Space Station?

The shift is welcome to many in that it hastened an end to "benching" and completely open offices, design ideas that were intended to increase collaboration (and save money on real estate) but frequently did the opposite. Harvard Business School professor Ethan Bernstein and Humanyze CEO Ben Waber found that face-to-face interactions *dropped* by roughly 70 percent after two Fortune 500 firms transitioned to open offices, while electronic interactions increased to compensate.[22] Early research showed that a small minority of employees wanted to continue to work exclusively from home. People missed impromptu face-to-face interaction and the feeling of community attached to a workplace.[23]

Our teams have learned that staying connected while working apart is much easier when we remember to ease up on our work personas a little. We've had practice because our teams have been virtual for years, but it was helpful and healthy to add time at the beginning of every meeting for a quick check-in like the ones we described in Chapter 8—a few minutes to acknowledge that we were working in unprecedented times, that there were new pressures and difficulties, from caring for children without daycare help to losing friends or family members to illness. In the past, we were proud of finishing our calls early. It showed efficiency and energy. Now we deliberately run over because people need to talk. If a team member really needed more support than time would allow, the meeting leader would suggest the call run long with those who could stay on the line, or the team leader would support the suffering member privately and connect the person with Deloitte resources.

Working from home often deprives people of habitual signals they have in offices to take a break, and we've seen people who went straight from a commute and a lunch break to sitting in front of screens 9 or 11 hours a day. The work just sucks you in. But self-care is not selfish. A healthy alternative is to consider the time you used to spend commuting as bonus time. Dedicate that time to exercise or meditation or reading or playing with your pets or children. It will build the resilience people need when they have to adapt to change. It will create an opportunity out of adversity. It's a small bit of healthy compensation for adjusting to the virtual world.

An unexpected upside to constant teleconferencing was that we became more conscious of our video backgrounds or turned off the video because we'd just come in from working out. Jen initially thought she had to get dressed up in her professional uniform for video meetings, but as more people showed up wearing their "pandemic outfits," the group talked about letting go of that pretense. Now, when people need to meet right after her workout, she just tells them, "I'm going to have my headband on, and I'll be chugging water and eating a snack, but let's go with it." There's some beauty found in that attitude because we're signaling that this is real life and it's *not* normal. People chuckled when they saw a big face from below, with a large blob intruding on the picture as people fiddled with video controls on a tablet. People heard a child's voice and said, "That's okay; go see what your child wants."

Now the team has the freedom to show up with kittens meowing in the background or with dogs barking at the mail carrier or delivery person. The work gets done anyway, and with all its informality, each team member is welcome to open a little window into who they are outside the office. It's an affirmation that when home became the office, it didn't stop being home.

We became conscious that even the most helpful teleconferencing apps change our behavior. We would never bring a mirror to a meeting in a conference room . . . but it's natural to look at ourselves during a virtual meeting. We learned to spend some meetings only in audio mode, or call in. And when someone else spoke, we tried to look directly into the camera—just that bit of artificial eye contact made a difference.

We also learned to safely bend the rules of social distancing. One of us even met up with a local team member for a check-in outdoors at a coffee shop. We found a giant picnic table and just chatted about our work. That short face-to-face was a highlight of the week for both of us.

There were parts of our lives that we previously had never shared, even in our virtual offices. Someone would notice all the Harry Potter books on someone's bookshelf, or the ancient maps framed on a team member's wall, or what someone selected for a virtual background. Humanizing people in a difficult situation is a perfect signal that while systems matter, people matter more.

KEY POINTS

- We have adopted information technology far faster than we have adapted to it.
- Work technology based on social media design is compelling, but magnifies social media's design drawbacks, including its addictive qualities and propensity to magnify emotional states.
- Taking deliberate small steps, like a weeklong digital detox, can return us to greater control over our technology use.
- Living and working virtually through teleconferencing invites us to adjust our behavior from bureaucratic, "professional" personas to intentionally more empathetic, caring interactions.

CHAPTER 10

LEADING THE CHANGE

Human knowledge is never contained in one person.
It grows from the relationships we create between each
other and the world, and still it is never complete.

—Paul Kalanithi, *When Breath Becomes Air*

You can be part of the change toward a culture that nurtures strong, meaningful relationships and well-being—whatever your position in your organization. Especially if you are a leader in any capacity, helping the people you lead build that culture should be one of your highest priorities. All the human skills that drive great performance depend on strong relationships to thrive and well-being to endure.

It's a process that happens on individual, team, and organizational levels simultaneously. Four stages describe the human side of managing change. First, individuals need *awareness* that there's a need for change and an intention to address it. Second, people *assimilate* that information in a personal way—"Here's what well-being means to me and my team." Knowing that, people move into *action*, trying out new behaviors individually and as a group. Fourth, the commitment and positive results turn people toward *advocacy*, in which they bring their well-being message and insights to the organization at large (and sometimes beyond that to communities, families, and other groups). The cycle of awareness, assimilation, action, and advocacy is common to all kinds of change. Sometimes it means developing the habits to live a healthier lifestyle. Sometimes it means changing how we work in our teams. And sometimes it means acquiring a whole new understanding of the connections between work and well-being.

For leaders, the cycle is personal and is also played out on the larger stage of the organization, and this is true whether one is bringing a Trusted Teams ethic to the organization or implementing a new technology. All change needs champions, strategists, communicators, and advocates on an ongoing basis—and these roles come together in leadership. You must be clear about the goal and committed to a strategy that gives adequate resources to achieve that goal. You must demonstrate personal commitment by your actions as well as your words. You must make well-being a strategic priority.

Fortunately, the journey toward organizational well-being fits well with the changes business has undergone in the last 20 years. Well-being is interdependent, requiring people of all kinds to understand and leverage their differences and diversity for the good of all. It requires a wide range of skills and collective innovation. Practically, it means piloting many different solutions and ideas and gathering feedback, discarding pet ideas and bureaucracy in the interest of implementing new and better ways of working together.

A Vision for Well-Being

An enduring change in organizational culture happens both top down and bottom up. Leaders can describe a vision, and that vision becomes reality as employees integrate the vision into day-to-day work, even as they continue to handle their regular jobs.[1] (This is another way of saying, "Build well-being into the flow of work.")

Employees only know a vision is truly important when leaders pursue it with intentionality. That means directing action, strategy, values, and the organization's mission toward a vision of well-being. While that might seem abstract, it's absolutely critical that leaders create a vision of well-being that they will commit to and demonstrate, day in and day out, in their own behavior.

A vision for well-being is grounded in your organization's authentic mission and culture, and it must be clear and simple to understand. That doesn't mean its wording has to be workshopped for months until you have it perfectly right. It means employees should be able to describe what well-being means to them and their group. It means everyone knows what good relationships and teamwork and trust look like. It means people know what behaviors are acceptable or unacceptable, and what behaviors contribute to the growth and realization of well-being for all.

Your well-being vision should:

- Give people the support and flexibility to make daily choices that allow them to be energized, confident, and aware.
- Empower people to personalize their experiences in the ways that matter most to them when it comes to their physical, mental, and financial well-being, as well as their sense of purpose.
- Create a well-being culture and people experience that promotes courageous conversations around mental health—

by encouraging vulnerability, tolerance, and empathy, allowing for the removal of stigma and supporting a more resilient workforce.

Creating a culture of Trusted Teams requires similar commitment from the top and similar autonomy throughout the organization. Well-being cannot be the sole responsibility of the HR department (or even a CHRO). Getting there as an organization is a change management effort, and like other change management it requires everyone's participation.

Successful change management involving culture like this must be highly programmatic, supported at all levels of the organization, planned across all departments, and sustained over time. We've seen well-being efforts fail when companies throw a lot of money at well-being tools, resources, and programs without a full development strategy, and without it being integrated into their talent life cycle strategy. We've shown that the most successful programs drive well-being into the flow of work. Likewise, the change management programs to create well-being are embedded into the norms and values that define organizational culture.

How does this happen? It happens when you win the hearts and minds of employees by making well-being personal. What are people going to get out of it? How will integrating well-being into the flow of work affect their closest team relationships? How will they advocate for themselves and others, mutually supporting one another with a shared language and beliefs about every person's right to personal well-being? When employees understand that, when they share a language about values and expectations, it changes their behavior, and that over time is what changes the real culture of the organization.

We saw great examples of cultures responding to change during the COVID-19 pandemic. For example:

- A distiller that quickly retooled one of its facilities to make hand sanitizer.[2]
- A sports equipment manufacturer that pivoted to making personal protective equipment such as face shields for healthcare workers.[3]
- The automobile companies that retooled plants to make ventilators and masks.[4]

These pivots are complex, requiring coordination and innovative action from every corner of companies—financial analysts, designers, supply chain managers, IT, and others.

Well-being, like other types of cultural change, don't happen overnight. Cultural change takes time because it's about changing beliefs and habits and emotions, and human beings just aren't very quick to do that. People always weigh trade-offs, even ones that they might not be aware of at first. Every team considers how to move toward well-being and better relationships from where they are at this moment. Some will move faster, some slower, and overall progress should be measured in daily experiences as well as long-term metrics like employee health, retention, and engagement.

For example, how can a person who has spent years believing that she has to work longer hours than anyone else in the group, because she is its leader, feel comfortable saying, "I'm going away for two weeks; don't contact me"?

This happened to Jen when she went on vacation. Discussing last-minute items on a team call, she was surprised when one of the members said, "Jen, email is your weakness, so we're just not going to send you emails while you're on vacation. Are you okay with that?"

Jen recalls, "I *said* I was totally okay with it, but inside I was thinking, wow, how am I going to handle this? How will I know what's going on? But my team was determined to support my well-being: They were going to force me to disconnect.

"When I got back, everything was fine, of course. They'd managed well without me. I sent them all a big thank you, because they had done what we need to do as people, as leaders, and as team members need to do—hold each other accountable and help each other with positive adaptation to the temptations of technology."

Jen already knew all the reasons to disconnect, but old habits are old habits, and they are very hard to change.

Workforce well-being is best understood as strategic investments, and so you look at progress along preplanned metrics. Put in financial terms, a strong well-being strategy shows growth over a matter of years, not just quarter to quarter.

The Role of the C-Suite

While a well-being strategy traditionally is typically managed by a chief human resources officer, we've recently seen programs partnering with chief people officers, who in large organizations are responsible for the entire talent life cycle from planning and recruiting for a superior workforce, through career planning, growth and learning, diversity and inclusion, and succession planning. But responsibility for well-being should be built into the strategic goals of all leaders, congruent with their roles.

Geoff McDonald, cofounder of Minds@Work, says responsibility for well-being belongs at the top: "My question to every CEO, every leader out there is, 'why is health *not* a strategic priority in your organization?' If it's not a strategic priority, it doesn't get the financial and the human resource that is required to execute that strategic priority. And it should be a strategic priority because it's the most important driver of performance."[5]

McDonald likens the integration of well-being to technology integration: If you make a major investment in infrastructure, you don't just employ it one or two weeks a year and then go back to the old way of doing things. You build a companywide change management program to make the most of your investment. Embracing and implementing well-being is no less rewarding or challenging.

Here's a high-level guide of roles and responsibilities for the C-suite:

> *CEO (chief executive officer).* Creates an organization-wide understanding that well-being is a vital component of the overall strategy, to be embraced as completely as other transformative movements like agility and continuous learning. Sets an example with public well-being habits. Establishes key performance indicators for well-being in the workforce.
>
> *CHRO (chief human resources officer)/CPO (chief people officer).* Assumes the operating charge of the long-term well-being strategy (or even better, works toward the establishment of a chief well-being officer in charge of permanent well-being programs). Invests in ways to take a constant pulse of employee needs and cultural transformation through current and predictive analytics. Integrates well-being into the employer brand. Strategizes with other leaders to bring well-being programs into all other organization-wide systems (IT, learning, etc.).
>
> *CIO (chief information officer).* Designs/builds/buys technology to promote, track, and manage well-being programs that are integrated into other systems such as CRM and communications technologies. Joins with well-being leadership to diagnose and describe how work technologies might

negatively impact well-being (through overuse or the habits described in Chapter 9).

CFO (chief financial officer). Establishes and monitors financial and productivity metrics affected by well-being programs. Quantifies the financial costs and benefits of a continued, long-term investment in well-being programs and connects these to the bottom line.

CRO (chief risk officer). Manages the increased focus on personal data, protecting privacy while supplying relevant data about the workforce overall. Mitigates risk by integrating well-being apps into overall data protection safeguards.

CMO (chief marketing officer). Positions well-being as a critical component of the employer brand externally and employee experience internally. Works with the CHRO to establish well-being as part of total rewards, and works with the CFO for messaging about how well-being contributes to financial performance.

These are strategic actions for the different disciplines of the C-suite. Once again, we come back to the power of the example set by senior leadership, and that always comes down to creating a human story.

"Every leader has to start by understanding what it means to be a caring leader," says George Kohlrieser, distinguished professor of leadership and organizational behavior at the International Institute for Management Development in Switzerland. "For years, caring was seen as a weakness, but now we know that the best way to get a result is to care about people, [to say] 'I'm here to help, I'm here to serve' [and] define the meaning and purpose of what they're doing."[6]

Cultural Cues

The C-suite also models cultural cues that encourage well-being, and these will vary according to the company's authentic culture.

First, people (at any level) must define individually what their well-being "nonnegotiables" are, according to the self-understanding we discussed earlier. Maybe that's sleep and exercise, or it could be open, honest, and direct dialogues with key team members. It could be time with family or community, switched off from work.

Here are five ways any team leader can contribute broadly to well-being programs:

1. *Encourage open conversations.* Focus on creating a safe workplace where people feel comfortable speaking openly about physical, relational, and mental health. Offer different avenues for personal conversation—openly in teams or in confidence with resources like a counselor.

2. *Make rest and recovery a priority.* At different points in the year, encourage large populations to disconnect together to allow everyone time for rest and recovery. Make it a point of culture that people can also choose time off when they need it. Check that rest and recovery time is used by everyone, with equity and as much personal choice as possible.

3. *Build mental health literacy.* Add virtual courses in mental health to the learning program so that everyone is conversant and comfortable with the issues. It's a topic many find distressing because of old cultural stigmas or personal anxiety. A well-being program treats mental health with candor, offering resources, tools, and educational opportunities to help people who are suffering.

4. *Support healthy habits.* Offer a well-being subsidy to help offset the costs of well-being–related products and services, like meditation instruction, yoga classes, and fees associated with gyms, hiking trails, charitable runs, horseback riding, and more.

5. *Share through storytelling.* Teach employees to share their experiences related to mental health and tell their stories in their own words. These stories are shared and promoted throughout the organization, and they are a great exercise in team bonding.

Modeling Behavior

Modeling healthy behaviors and telling personal stories about well-being send a powerful message, and leadership must send that message openly and often. That calls for a more personal touch than many would be comfortable with, but it's critical to the success of any well-being program.

Susan David, author of *Emotional Agility*, points out that some of our most difficult emotions are signals that can take us into deeper understanding of a situation. She told us, "I have never met someone who is depressed, who isn't concerned about how they can better participate. I have never met someone who is anxious socially, who isn't concerned at some level about how they can better show up in the world. If someone is bored, the value that that negative feeling might be pointing to is a desire to grow and learn."[7]

You create emotional granularity—bypassing the usual conversation that goes, "How are you?" "I'm fine," by taking time to understand where people are in their work or their lives. A good time to do this is at the beginning of a meeting. For a few minutes, have people share not *what* they're doing but *how* they're doing. (For that matter, meetings that consist of status updates are a poor use of everyone's time. Team leaders can improve efficiency simply by requiring status updates be made before the meeting through collaboration platforms. The time saved can be dedicated to the things meetings do well, like collaborating on ideas and brain-storming solutions.)

The team leader models behavior by answering the opening question thoughtfully. Questions that can reveal our whole selves might be:

- What concerns you most about our work at this moment?
- What are you most confident about in your part of this project?
- What do you want to bring to this meeting, and what do you want to leave behind?
- What are you learning this week?

Keep answers short—just a few words. If issues arise that need deeper discussion or resolution, that's a good use of meeting time.

The high-stakes issue of mental health is growing as a concern among employees, and normalizing the conversation around it is critical to improving addressing mental health problems like burn-out, depression, anxiety, addiction, and the disengagement that results from these problems. The truly self-confident leader finds a way to share his or her experiences with an understanding of well-being, including the parts that aren't so easy to tell. Research shows that when executives share their experiences (or those of friends or family members) dealing with mental health challenges, they decrease the cultural harm. Researchers wrote recently in the *Harvard Business Review* that "modeling disclosure and vulnerability as strengths, not weaknesses, goes a long way toward reducing the stigma and setting the tone for transparency."[8]

The same is true of normalizing other well-being conversations, including talking about rest, recreation, stress, the habituating nature of our technologies, and even the toll that bureaucracy takes on people. These conversations might already be happening in private during work or over after-work drinks, but that very avoidance perpetuates the silence that gives mental health its stigma. When leaders create a safe and welcoming culture for negative as well as positive emotions, individuals feel empowered to speak up and ask for help.

We practice this with our own teams. We've learned to say, "I'm feeling really stressed out by this setback in that project," just to put the reality of our feelings out there. Other team members have permission to do the same. When we hear this from another member, we might go around the table asking if others feel that way, or we might make a mental note to follow up later with the individual who is stressed or suffering, remembering that one of our most important jobs as leaders is to help remove all roadblocks to progress. That doesn't mean we can or should "solve" the problem every time; it means we can see the situation clearly and take action at the appropriate time. If we know someone's struggling, we'll have a private conversation, saying we can see the struggle and suggesting how we can help. Most of those conversations involve a lot of listening on our part, because people are reluctant to show their difficulties or feel like a drag on the team, even in times of great stress.

Some of our favorite questions are:

- How are you sleeping?
- How can I support you?
- What are your top three feelings today?
- What have you done just for yourself today?
- What story are you telling yourself today?
- How are you, really?
- What are you grateful for?

When you ask a specific question like this, you can offer specific resources to help, even if the problem is different from the one you suspect. For example, you might ask someone if he's getting enough sleep, to which he answers yes, but he's really stressed about making healthcare decisions for an aging parent. Knowing this, you can encourage him to use resources in an employee referral program to discuss money, healthcare, or stress issues. Asking, waiting, listening, and offering help in the form of corporate well-being resources will give people permission to drop the persona that says "Everything's fine." Understanding what people might be struggling with also provides context for how they might be showing up at work.

One of the hardest habits to break is a 24/7 work ethic. Harvard Business School professor Leslie Perlow, author of *Sleeping with Your Smartphone,* found that teams can improve well-being when they establish collective goals. For example, her research found that when the members of a team each chose a preselected night off from work, and they committed to covering for each other, they were able to stick to the resolution and in fact outperformed teams of always-on individuals.[9] Partners help us stick to our goals and stay accountable for changing our habits for the better (as members of support groups like Weight Watchers can readily attest).

Leaders communicate which boundaries between work and nonwork life are their priorities, and then ask others to also share what their particular boundaries are. People have their own pressure points, whether that's working too many hours, or having a terrible commute, or being expected to answer emails quickly, or being interrupted too often.

We've all been told to hide our emotions at work, but that message can cut us off from one another. It also leads to toxic interactions as people lose their tempers or blame or play the victim. Open, honest, and direct conversation about how we're doing is a sign of maturity; showing up as our whole selves builds confidence in a person and within a team.

In their insightful book, *Time Off,* John Fitch and Max Frenzel coined the wonderful term "rest ethic," playing off "work ethic" to describe the need to build routines of mental and physical rest into our lives. Frenzel told us that even in a telemeeting there are ways to promote a rest ethic. He said, "Change things up! Ask each person on your team, 'What are you doing in your free time, or what activities did you get into this weekend?' Then investigate further and ask them *why* they do that. You'll see people's eyes light up because you're honoring what makes them interesting. That is the lifeblood of creativity and enthusiasm."[10]

A Framework for Well-Being

As senior leaders help bring well-being into work's design by modeling behavior and investing in well-being programs, they should elevate well-being to the status of any other factor that affects the company's performance. That means that the program is strategic and that team leaders are expected to treat it as an organizational priority.

Team leaders have the power to connect program elements to the reality of everyone's jobs. Their role as connectors is critical to managing the performance of the group as a whole. As coaches and mentors, team leaders require their members to understand and honor each individual's well-being. That's another signal of the importance of the program, and it helps the group perform better.

Individuals are not passive recipients of well-being; they must determine their own well-being needs, set their own boundaries, and participate in the development of flexible and responsive policies and actions. Individually and with others, people need to find that right balance of personal needs and those of the team and the organization—a conversation that can enrich the program and relationships among team members.

Organizations should also take into account the environments in which they're designing work, as work increasingly crosses cultures, geographies, functions, and physical and virtual workspaces. The suggestions below offer a starting point for leaders to think through what changes they can make in five environments across the three levels (the bulleted points are specific recommendations for different levels):

Cultural

Building well-being into social behaviors and norms

- *Organizations.* Model well-being behaviors such as taking microbreaks or only making certain meetings video-focused.
- *Individuals.* Be proactive and vocal about well-being needs.

Relational

Fostering well-being in relationships among colleagues

- *Organizations.* Form teams based on worker preferences, working styles, and personal needs in addition to skill sets.
- *Individuals.* Check in frequently, proactively, and consistently with colleagues on their well-being needs and preferences.

Operational

Including well-being in management policies, processes, and programs

- *Organizations.* Embed well-being criteria in work scheduling, performance management processes, leadership evaluations, and rewards and recognition programs.
- *Teams.* Enable team agency and choice by allowing teams to adopt the well-being practices best suited to them.

Physical

Designing the physical workspace to facilitate well-being

- *Organizations.* Design work environments to support workers' physical, mental, and emotional health needs.
- *Teams.* Leverage physical workspaces that promote team collaboration and performance.

Virtual

Designing new technologies and virtual workspaces for well-being

- *Organizations.* Use new technologies, like virtual reality, to train team members to navigate stressful situations (e.g., interacting with a frustrated customer).
- *Individuals.* Leverage wearable technologies and apps to help master distractions, increase mindfulness, and reduce anxiety.

When an organization is able to successfully design well-being into work, well-being becomes indistinguishable from work itself and embedded across all organizational levels and environments so that it drives and sustains not only human performance but also human potential.[11]

Tech—Lead by Example

Unintended consequences accompany new technology, as we've seen so starkly with social media and other platforms in which we invest our personas. We begin by using apps to collaborate, but before long we're creating an image. We lose track of how fast or how late at night we reply to email or how often we suggest a new idea. We lose empathy and jump to conclusions about another person's intent or tone, momentarily forgetting that email is an imperfect medium.

A new work technology might come with a training video or guide, but you never know exactly how you'll end up using it. Humans are incredibly creative with their technology. Anh and her coauthors in *The Technology Fallacy* point out the classic example of duct tape, which was originally designed for use in WWII, and then to hold ducts in HVAC systems together but now has literally thousands of uses. Closer to the office, we notice the trend that all our devices are becoming interoperable. Take a picture with your phone and send it via a message app to a cloud-based sharing platform, where a team member can use powerful video editing software on a PC to alter the picture and email it to others—and so on. As we've seen, all this power and sharing is also habituating, and also intrusive unless we build up our power to use tech with intentionality. We need to separate the ways we *can* use tech from the ways we *should* use it.[12]

Here's a simple example: One day while we were collaborating remotely on this book, Jen received a four-paragraph message via instant message from a colleague overseas. The message laid out a complex meeting topic and asked for an immediate response. Instant messaging connotes an urgency about the communication, but there was nothing urgent about the request. In fact, it required careful consideration. In that moment, Jen chose not to respond, and later she asked the colleague to resend the request in email, promising to get to it in an appropriate time frame.

That was just one interaction, but the technology used wasn't right for the purpose intended. Fill the day with "urgent" interactions, and you create a situation in which nothing can take priority. Jen's response maintained the boundary between urgent and routine.

Special mention goes to the habit we've seen (and fallen into ourselves) of carrying out group conversations over text when a simple call would be far more efficient. Setting a boundary on this kind of habitual behavior can be as simple as texting, "Let's have a call on this," instead of continuing an endless thread of text messages.

Finally, team leaders should emphasize that everyone can contribute. More than setting boundaries with collaboration technology, leaders can solicit suggestions for working better together. Often, the newest team member can approach the work routine with fresh eyes, especially if the person is coming into the team from a different department or a different company.

KEY POINTS

- Leaders begin by articulating a vision for well-being, connected to the values and mission of the organization.
- Managers, team leaders, and other employees start their well-being habits in their immediate teams, practicing new behaviors with those they trust most.
- Leaders at all levels must model well-being habits themselves, telling stories and being explicit about their personal "nonnegotiable" habits and boundaries.
- A long-term well-being program is strategic and measures success in improved human capital metrics over years, not months.

SEEING OURSELVES AND EACH OTHER

We go to the Internet for information.
We go to human beings to learn.

—Ken Blanchard[1]

"In South Africa, where I come from, there is a Zulu greeting you hear on the streets every day," says Professor Susan David. "It's a beautiful word, *sawubona*. It means hello but when translated literally it means 'I see you.' When leaders use it, they mean 'I recognize that what you feel is real.'"

The customary reply to "Sawubona" is "Yebo sawubona," which means "I see you seeing me." It implies "When you recognize me in all my full humanity, I recognize you too, and I honor your acknowledgment of me."

If we were to distill the message of this book to a single word, it would be "sawubona." We must see each other in our complexity, our uniqueness, and our common ground, to form strong relationships at work and to nurture well-being in ourselves and our teams. And when we are faced with a choice between these and less healthy work habits and attitudes, we must consciously choose the former.

It takes courage to follow this path, because even though we might want greater well-being and a work life that aligns with our values, we face constant trade-offs and temptations to behave in unhealthy ways. We become habituated to pursuing the next milestone on the way to achievement or security in whatever form it takes for us. We want the rewards of money, property, and position, but when a goal is achieved, we habitually look to the next milestone, until we find we have spent years pursuing ever-receding goals, rather than being our most authentic and healthy selves right now. We compromise our behavior a little bit at a time; we might be uncertain of which values reflect our authentic selves. We stay on the traditional path because the rewards it offers are worthy and valuable, and because we are aware of the risks of changing ourselves. We might fail. We might fall short. We might alienate someone. We might get fired.

And yet . . . we who are lucky enough to even make a choice have the option to pour our energies into the creation of a better world right in our own workplaces, seeing each other and putting our common well-being first.

Relationships at work are dynamic, changing with the business landscape, or our personal situations. How many people from your first or second job are you still in contact with, and have those relationships changed? If you're like most of us, the answers are "just a few" and "of course."

Relationships that make it possible for people to achieve their maximum potential well-being will always require commitment, empathy, compromise, and shared values. Nobody will negotiate the complex web of relationships perfectly, including those at work. Nor would we want anyone to be perfect at this work. We (Jen and Anh) have made plenty of mistakes as we moved ahead with our teams and organizations. But perfection isn't the goal: acknowledging, accepting, and growing from those missteps is our aspiration, because that helps us all become more human.

Changing a culture, like other change management, means never standing still. There's no time when you get to say we have achieved well-being for everyone and established great team relationships, because you need to think of these like other strategic goals as a trendline and incremental steps in the unfolding of the history of your organization.

"Seeing each other" at work takes time and carries surprises along the way. We came by separate paths to our understanding of the ideas in this book, and in both our cases it was a matter of steady progress, not revolution.

ANH

I did not anticipate this when I started my career, but over the years I've grown steadily to appreciate the power of relationships. As I dug into the psychology and research on human connection, I've seen that it transcends boundaries between work and home, or work and community. Studying relationships at work made me rethink all my personal relationships to really understand how it all fits together. It's elevated my perspective that human connection is valuable in all parts of my life.

In 2020, the pandemic has made it harder to connect with people, but instead of retreating into my own nuclear family bubble, I made an effort to stay connected and to reach out to people I hadn't connected to in a while. At the same time, I put some boundaries around relationships that weren't entirely healthy for me, and I might not have done that if the pandemic hadn't raised my awareness of what makes for well-being both in and out of work.

JEN

Diving into the topics covered in this book with research and the conversations we've quoted, I've also seen that many people are not very good at separating life and work. I'm a "subject-matter expert" in well-being, but I'm still impressed at the mountain of evidence accumulating that shows close personal relationships are the number one factor determining long-term health. Loneliness—lack of connection—literally kills people.

Thankfully, the opposite is also true. I've seen confirmation that positive relationships are good for our physical and mental health. For me, positive relationships increase my capacity for empathy, kindness, and self-compassion. When I weigh how much energy I want to put into a relationship, I want to commit that time more to relationships that "fill my cup." Kindness in a workplace ripples outward and benefits more than just me (and the opposite, unkindness, also ripples outward, so I try to limit my interaction with people who aren't good for me).

I encourage the people with whom I work to do that too, and to remain open to greater self-awareness about their impact on others. In that way, this work has had a powerful effect on who I am as a person and who I am as a leader.

Setting limits on unhealthy relationships has made us better at our work and more tolerant of differences. Is that a contradiction? No, because setting limits on negative behavior in a team or one-to-one increases psychological safety. You can work effectively with someone without enabling the person to dominate or change you. Our stories also show that focusing on the positive relationships—or even the positive aspects of a nonideal relationship—improves our mental and even physical health.

The same is true for redeveloping a healthy relationship with work technology. Work-life integration includes learning to become more intentional about how much time and attention our technologies command. As we've seen, this is becoming harder as the conceptual and design differences between work and personal technologies blur.

The same is true for moving toward being more authentic and intentional, in a way that maintains appropriate boundaries such as personal privacy but also drops pretensions that don't reflect your deepest values. How we show up at work is a construct that takes its cues from a combination of organizational values and individual temperamental factors. When certain values—or their appearance—are rewarded, it's natural to act them out. That's why, for example, a person with a Pioneer temperament might take a position that requires a lot of attention to detail (not a Pioneer quality at all), because it's a promotion with more money, more responsibility, and greater prestige. When we say yes to an opportunity that conflicts with our authentic selves, we set the stage for burnout, frustration, or failure. (Promoting someone from skilled software engineer to unskilled and unhappy manager is a classic mistake.)

As you begin the work of improving relationships at work, you might have doubts. You will get pushback from those internal voices that say, "They don't have time or inclination to change." . . . "They won't take me seriously." . . . They won't cooperate." . . . "They won't respect me."

To those voices we have a simple answer: "I can't control *they*, but I can control *me*."

Start with your own willingness to promote your well-being at work and to remain true to your values. And then find allies who also want to improve the workplace. When you have just a few like-minded people working together, you all can say, "We can't control *they*, but we can control *we*."

Start with the Big Ideas

The main ideas in this book, the ones that bring people closer toward sawubona, are dualities with a feeling of tension between them. For example, we began this book by noting that we are more connected than ever, and yet loneliness is epidemic. Work technology makes us more productive, and yet its habituating design leads to overuse and addiction, when we become less productive.

Given these dualities, the path forward to strong relationships and well-being is to become more intentional about what we do and to make a commitment to ground all our behaviors, individually and as teams, in carefully chosen values.

Review these dualities as you examine your own situation, both personally and on your teams:

> *Recognize that both problems and solutions are empowered by our attitudes toward them.* When we accept parts of organizational culture that hurt relationships or well-being, we give them power to degrade our teams and our health. When we insist on positive values and behaviors, we improve relationships and well-being (and in the process, improve performance).

> *Understand your own style, and exercise empathy to understand the styles of others.* The key to living authentically at work is identifying your own tendencies, strengths, temperament, and habits. The key to acting authentically as a group is recognizing and accepting diversity along the same lines, without judgment but taking advantage of differences.

> *Value strong relationships and individual well-being.* Strong relationships at work, which we call Trusted Teams, are founded in mutual respect and a common dedication to values that the group articulates and enforces. The group supports

individual well-being by accepting individual behaviors and accountability. Trust, belonging, engagement, knowledge sharing, and positivity are among the best indicators of strong relationships.

Set personal limits with technology; use tech to amplify relationships, not dilute them. People decide for themselves the degree to which their behavior with technology blurs the lines between work and life or positive and negative. Individuals then agree to use technology wisely and to mutually support each other's healthy behaviors. In particular, habits that break the alienating qualities of telework and remote teams support well-being.

To initiate change, start with yourself and then share your experiences to help change your team. Telling stories, sharing tips and techniques, bridging your different work styles to connect as humans, and checking in regularly with yourself and your team provide momentum to healthy changes at work.

Articulate a vision; lead by example; let go of control; iterate solutions. Leaders must express a vision for well-being and demonstrate constantly that they are walking the talk. Teams can design their best path to strong relationships and individual well-being within the context of an organization's culture. And leadership isn't limited to the top of the org chart or the project lead; anyone can highlight which team solutions work and help communicate them to all.

Remember that work-life integration does not equal always working. The lines between work and life will continue to blur in the coming years, especially as work routines change in response to the pandemic and post-pandemic. Thus, work-life integration becomes part of everyone's jobs, to prevent their own burnout and maintain healthy team relationships.

Be Your Own Chief Well-Being Officer

Part Three of this book, "People First, Systems Second," emphasized that creating well-being in ourselves and our teams is a long-
term job. Summing up the task of well-being from many angles,
we formulated the following points we try to remember all the
time. Think of these points as a checklist for being your own chief
well-being officer.[2]

Take a holistic approach to well-being. Your physical and
mental health, relationships, sense of purpose, and financial
health all affect your overall well-being. Some people add
spiritual and community health to that list. Choose the most
important changes you'd like to make over the next year or two
for each, and check in with a trusted friend to examine if the
goals are both realistic and authentic to your true values.

Set priorities. Jen likes to ask, "What are your nonnegotiables?"
For some it will be exercise; for others, time with family; and
for others, time to pursue interests outside of work. The
specific item matters less than that you choose to put it before
others. Another way to ask this is, "If a new job offer included a
guarantee that my nonnegotiables would be respected, what
would be my top three?" Check in with your goals every six
months (put it on the calendar).

Involve others. We encourage the members of our teams to
share their well-being and relationship values with each other,
and we regularly remind ourselves that "Well-being is #1."
Sharing also allows team members to support each other in
their goals and values.

Schedule it. You make time for work. You schedule meetings
and deadlines. Well-being activities and habits are just as

valuable. You can start by scheduling daily reminders of the activities in the "digital detox" in Chapter 9.

Fail well. You're going to skip a day of exercise, or eat a pint of ice cream one evening while watching your favorite show. There's no point in beating yourself up about "slips," because they'll happen and setbacks are part of the process. The next day, get back to the routine.

Find joy and give thanks. Leave space in your day for the activities, things, or people that give you joy. Make a habit of expressing gratitude, in whatever form works for you. Especially, express gratitude to the people at work for the good things they bring to your life. Gratitude is one of the fundamental habits of well-being.

Become an Advocate

There are times at work when everyone is working in harmony—when well-being and healthy relationships are part of the daily routine, you feel authentic connection, and the team produces great work.

Those are times to enjoy, and also to remember that the job of connection is never done. No matter how good you are at relationships, there's always room for growth, and—because you are human—you'll mess up somewhere along the way. Living in the middle of constant change, and constant demands for attention from people and technology, you still have to be alert to the human tendency toward habituation and routine—or worse, falling into behaviors that are inconsistent with your values in times of stress. That takes an alert kind of energy, as well as understanding that there is no such thing as a perfect, permanent solution.

The work we've described in this book benefits from the "network effect," a term economists use for the phenomenon that "the more people use it, the more valuable it becomes." The internet is the prime example—once an obscure set of protocols used by the military and scientists, its emergence as a worldwide network in the 1990s made it invaluable to modern life. In the same way, the more people in an organization put well-being and strong, authentic relationships at the forefront of their work, the more effective well-being and authenticity become in their ability to promote traditional measures of value, like profits, innovation, and engagement.

What if an organization created incentives to help people feel their best, in the same way it uses incentives to get people to perform their best? What if objective measures of well-being were pursued as ardently as quarterly profit numbers, employee engagement scores, or best-in-class company ratings? Obviously, that organization would spend less on health and recruiting costs; as we've seen, productivity and innovation and agility would increase. And when the next crisis hits, that organization would be more resilient and more capable of change.

For that to happen, people need to go beyond themselves and their teams and become advocates for every kind of well-being. Your journey must start with your own health (in every sense of that word) and the health and trust of the people on your team, but it doesn't end there. The ideas in this book are intended to empower people to advocate for these changes—to experiment, observe, amend, and advocate across the organization for a better way of being with each other.

Culture is what people experience day in, day out, through their collective words and actions. When everyone has the vision and vocabulary of well-being, every day presents opportunities to promote it. Every team meeting is a chance to strengthen the trust, authenticity, and productivity of the team.

You don't have to be a team leader to advocate for change. Be a role model in whatever group you participate. Invest your energy in your team, whether it's a squad of 5 participating in a teleconference or a department of 50 working on a complex project. Everyone has a role to play regardless of the person's formal influence on the organization chart. You might not set the strategic culture of your organization by giving directions, but you definitely contribute to the culture of your team with every interaction.

Human connection is the heart of who we are as people. It defines and regulates our relationships with family, friends, and colleagues. We rely heavily on the physical, spiritual, and emotional bonds we create with one another—their importance cannot be overstated. With physical distancing, we are losing opportunities for many of the physical components of human connection—eye contact, facial expressions, hand gestures, hugs, and hand shake, for example—that have been part of our everyday life for as long as any of us can remember. During the COVID-19 pandemic we were reminded of this every day. Physical distancing opened our eyes to just how much we need and want real human connection.

"Sawubona" means coming fully into a relationship with each other. We are always engaged with our fellow people in work, in family, and in community, and that engagement comes with the permanent responsibility to choose how we will be. Choose to be well. Choose to help others around you be well. Choose to create relationships you believe in with your whole heart, because that's the way to success in every corner of your life.

SUGGESTED READING

We are both nonstop readers, and so any list of books that have influenced our thinking about relationships and well-being is necessarily incomplete. The following are both excellent resources and relevant to the issues raised in *Work Better Together.* Many of the authors have joined Jen in her *WorkWell* podcast, which you can find at https://www2.deloitte.com/us/en/pages/about-deloitte/articles/workwell-podcast-series.html.

Atomic Habits: An Easy & Proven Way to Build Good Habits & Break Bad Ones, by James Clear

The Best Place to Work: The Art and Science of Creating an Extraordinary Workplace, by Ron Friedman

Bring Your Human to Work: 10 Surefire Ways to Design a Workplace That's Good for People, Great for Business, and Just Might Change the World, by Erica Keswin

Emotional Agility: Get Unstuck, Embrace Change and Thrive in Work and Life, by Susan David

Essentialism: The Disciplined Pursuit of Less, by Greg McKeown

Fire Your Boss: Discover Work You Love Without Quitting Your Job, by Aaron McHugh

Grit: The Power of Passion and Perseverance, by Angela Duckworth

Happier Now: How to Stop Chasing Perfection and Embrace Everyday Moments (Even the Difficult Ones), by Nataly Kogan

How to Live a Good Life: Soulful Stories, Surprising Science, and Practical Wisdom, by Jonathan Fields

Irresistible: The Rise of Addictive Technology and the Business of Keeping Us Hooked, by Adam Alter

Making Work Human: How Human-Centered Companies Are Changing the Future of Work and the World, by Eric Mosley and Derek Irvine

The Mindful Day: Practical Ways to Find Focus, Calm, and Joy from Morning to Evening, by Laurie J. Cameron

Mindset: The New Psychology of Success, by Carol Dweck

The Optimistic Workplace: Creating an Environment That Energizes Everyone, by Shawn Murphy

The Power of Habit: Why We Do What We Do in Life and Business, by Charles Duhigg

The Power Paradox: How We Gain and Lose Influence, by Dacher Keltner

The Rabbit Effect: Live Longer, Happier, and Healthier with the Groundbreaking Science of Kindness, by Kelli Harding

Radical Candor: Be a Kick-Ass Boss Without Losing Your Humanity, by Kim Scott

The Technology Fallacy: How People Are the Real Key to Digital Transformation, by Gerald C. Kane, Anh Nguyen Phillips, Jonathan R. Copulsky, and Garth R. Andrus

Thrive: The Third Metric to Redefining Success and Creating a Life of Well-Being, Wisdom, and Wonder, by Arianna Huffington

Time Off: A Practical Guide to Building Your Rest Ethic and Finding Success Without the Stress, by John Fitch and Max Frenzel

Together: The Healing Power of Human Connection in a Sometimes Lonely World, by Vivek H. Murthy

Why We Sleep: Unlocking the Power of Sleep and Dreams, by Matthew Walker

Wolfpack: How to Come Together, Unleash Our Power, and Change the Game, by Abby Wambach

NOTES

Introduction

1. "How Having a Best Friend at Work Transforms the Workplace," Gallup, October 16, 2018.
2. "Workplace Burnout Survey: Burnout Without Borders," https://www2 .deloitte.com/us/en/pages/about-deloitte/articles/burnout-survey.html.
3. "The Social Enterprise at Work: Paradox as a Path Forward," *Deloitte 2020 Global Human Capital Trends*, p. 2.

Chapter 1

1. "Frederick Winslow Taylor," British Library, https://www.bl.uk/people/frederick -winslow-taylor. Accessed June 3, 2020.
2. Susan M. Heathfield, "What Exempt Employee Status Means," The Balance Careers, updated January 16, 2020, https://www.thebalancecareers.com/ exempt-employees-1918120. Accessed June 4, 2020.
3. Derek Thompson, "The Religion of Workism Is Making Americans Miserable," *The Atlantic*, February 24, 2019.
4. One often-cited study from Stanford University (John Pencavel) found that pro-ductivity per hour declines sharply after 50 hours of work in a week. See Kabir Sehgal and Deepak Chopra, "Stanford Professor: Working This Many Hours a Week Is Basically Pointless. Here's How to Get More Done—by Doing Less," CNBC, March 20, 2019, https://www.cnbc.com/2019/03/20/stanford-study -longer-hours-doesnt-make-you-more-productive-heres-how-to-get-more-done -by-doing-less.html. Accessed June 2, 2020.
5. Sarah Green Carmichael, "The Research Is Clear: Long Hours Backfire for People and for Companies," *Harvard Business Review*, August 19, 2015.
6. Daniel Rose, "That New Productivity Tool Is Stressing Out Your Team," *Fast Company*, July 14, 2019, https://www.fastcompany.com/90376152/ttechnology -and-stress-in-the-workplace. Accessed June 4, 2020.
7. Steve Glaveski, "10 Quick Tips for Avoiding Distractions at Work," *Harvard Business Review*, December 18, 2019.
8. "How Silicon Valley Made Work More Stressful," Knowledge@Wharton, February 13, 2019, https://knowledge.wharton.upenn.edu/article/silicon-valley -work-culture/. Accessed June 4, 2020.

9. Susan Weinschenk, "The True Cost of Multitasking," *Psychology Today*, September 18, 2012.

10. "Cellular Phone Use and Texting While Driving Laws," National Conference of State Legislatures, May 29, 2019.

11. Gloria Mark, UC Irvine, and Daniela Gudith and Ulrich Klocke, Humboldt University, "The Cost of Interrupted Work: More Speed and Stress," *Proceedings of the 2008 Conference on Human Factors in Computing Systems*, April 2008.

12. Martin Curley, "Twelve Principles for Open Innovation 2.0," *Nature*, May 17, 2016.

13. "Beyond Reskilling: Investing in Resilience for Uncertain Futures," *2020 Deloitte Global Human Capital Trends—The Social Enterprise at Work: Paradox as a Path Forward*, p. 73.

14. Cathy Engelbert and John Hagel, "Radically Open: Tom Friedman on Jobs, Learning, and the Future of Work," *Deloitte Review*, no. 21, July 2017, p. 105.

15. Josh Bersin, "Catch the Wave: The 21st-Century Career," *Deloitte Review*, no. 21, July 2017, p. 71.

16. Matt Sigelman, "By the Numbers: The Job Market for Data Science and Analytics," Burning Glass Technologies, February 10, 2017.

17. *Deloitte Insights Tech Trends 2020*, p. 6.

18. John Hagel, Jeff Schwartz, and Josh Bersin, "Navigating the Future of Work," *Deloitte Review*, no. 21, July 2017, p. 38.

19. "2020 Edelman Trust Barometer Global Report," p. 15.

20. "The Future of Work: What Do We Know?," OECD Employment Outlook 2019. Section 2.1.1.

21. "Crunch Mode: Programming to the Extreme—the Relationship Between Hours Worked and Productivity," Stanford University, https://cs.stanford.edu/people/eroberts/cs201/projects/crunchmode/econ-hours-productivity.html Accessed March 12, 2021.

22. "Crunch Mode: Programming to the Extreme—Factors Contributing to Decreased Productivity," Stanford University, https://cs.stanford.edu/people/eroberts/cs201/projects/crunchmode/econ-factors-decreased.html. Accessed June 2, 2020.

23. "Jeff Bezos: Why Getting 8 Hours of Sleep Is Good for Amazon Shareholders," Thrive Global, November 30, 2016.

24. Kapo Wong, Alan H. S. Chan, and S. C. Ngan, "The Effect of Long Working Hours and Overtime on Occupational Health: A Meta-analysis of Evidence from 1998 to 2018," *International Journal of Environmental Research and Public Health*, June 13, 2019.

25. Jon Johnson, "Negative Effects of Technology: What to Know," medically reviewed by Timothy J. Legg, Ph.D., CRNP, *Medical News Today*, February 25, 2020.

26. Julia Sklar, "'Zoom Fatigue' Is Taxing the Brain. Here's Why That Happens," *National Geographic*, April 24, 2020, https://www.nationalgeographic.com/science/2020/04/coronavirus-zoom-fatigue-is-taxing-the-brain-here-is-why-that-happens/. Accessed June 2, 2020.

Chapter 2

1. "Designing Work Environments for Digital Well-Being," *Deloitte Review*, no. 23, July 2018.

2. Heejung Chung, "Flexible Working Is Making Us Work Longer," Quartz, April 27, 2017, https://qz.com/765908/flexible-working-is-making-us-work-longer/.

3. Yuval Noah Harari, *21 Lessons for the 21st Century*, New York: Spiegel & Grau, p. 128 (e-book edition).

4. Julianne Holt-Lunstad, Timothy B. Smith, and J. Bradley Layton, "Social Relationships and Mortality Risk: A Meta-analytic Review," *PLOS Medicine*, July 27, 2010, https://doi.org/10.1371/journal.pmed.1000316. Accessed June 29, 2020.

5. Christian Hakulinen et al., "Social Isolation and Loneliness as Risk Factors for Myocardial Infarction, Stroke and Mortality: UK Biobank Cohort Study of 479,054 Men and Women," *BMJ Journals*, vol. 104, no. 18, July 1, 2019.

6. Amy C. Edmondson, *The Fearless Organization: Creating Psychological Safety in the Workplace for Learning, Growth and Innovation*, New York: Wiley, 2018, publisher's description, https://bit.ly/3dKYPyj. Accessed June 30, 2020.

7. Tessa West, "The Lies We Tell at Work—and the Damage They Do," *Wall Street Journal*, July 21. 2020.

8. Ben Wigert and Sangeeta Agrawal, "Employee Burnout, Part 1: The 5 Main Causes," Gallup, July 12, 2018.

9. "Burn-Out an 'Occupational Phenomenon': International Classification of Diseases," World Health Organization, May 28, 2019, https://www.who.int/mental_health/evidence/burn-out/en/. Accessed June 29, 2020.

10. Jennifer Moss, "When Passion Leads to Burnout," *Harvard Business Review*, July 1, 2019.

11. Wigert and Agrawal, "Employee Burnout, Part 1."

12. Ryan Pendell, "Millennials Are Burning Out," Gallup, July 19, 2018.

13. Vivek Murthy, "Work and the Loneliness Epidemic: Reducing Isolation at Work Is Good for Business," *Harvard Business Review*, September 2017.

14. Ibid.

15. "Cigna Takes Action to Combat the Rise of Loneliness and Improve Mental Wellness in America," press release accompanying report, January 23, 2020.

16. Dan Buettner, *The Blue Zones of Happiness: Lessons from the World's Happiest People*, Washington, DC: National Geographic Partners, 2017, p. 167.

17. Tom Rath and Jim Harter, "Your Friends and Your Social Well-Being," Gallup, August 19, 2010.

18. Liz Mineo, "Good Genes Are Nice, but Joy Is Better." *The Harvard Gazette*, April 11, 2017 [Anh's statement at WHL 2019].

19. Liz Mineo, "Good Genes Are Nice, but Joy Is Better," *Harvard Gazette*, April 11, 2017.

20. Shawn Achor, "The Happy Secret to Better Work," TED Talk, https://www.ted.com/talks/shawn_achor_the_happy_secret_to_better_work/transcript. Accessed June 29, 2020.

21. "The Secrets to Employee Engagement," Tiny Pulse, https://www.tinypulse .com/blog/the-secrets-to-employee-engagement-new-report. Accessed December 5, 2020.

22. "Getting Along with Co-workers May Prolong Life, Researchers Find," American Psychological Association, 2011.

23. "State of the American Manager," Gallup, 2015.

24. Joel Goh, Jeffrey Pfeffer, and Stefanos A. Zenios, "Workplace Stressors & Health Outcomes: Health Policy for the Workplace," *Behavioral Science & Policy*, Spring 2015.

25. Rob Cross, Reb Rebele, and Adam Grant, "Collaborative Overload," *Harvard Business Review*, January–February 2016.

26. Karyn Twaronite, "A Global Survey on the Ambiguous State of Employee Trust," *Harvard Business Review*, July 22, 2016.

27. "2020 Edelman Trust Barometer Global Report," p. 10.

28. Deloitte Global Millennial Survey 2019.

29. "2020 Edelman Trust Barometer Spring Update: Trust and the Covid-19 Pandemic."

30. Emma Seppälä, "Positive Teams Are More Productive," *Harvard Business Review*, March 18, 2015.

31. Jim Harter, "4 Factors Driving Record-High Employee Engagement in U.S.," Gallup, February 4, 2020. *Note:* Even when almost two-thirds of employees were not engaged, this represented a slight increase in engagement from 2018.

32. "What Is Employee Engagement and How Do You Improve It?," Gallup Workplace, https://www.gallup.com/workplace/285674/improve-employee -engagement-workplace.aspx#ite-285707. Accessed December 5, 2020.

33. "Loneliness and the Workplace: The 2020 Report," Cigna.

34. "The Future of Work: What Do We Know?," OECD Employment Outlook 2019, Section 2.3.6.

Chapter 3

1. "Putting Meaning Back into Work," LinkedIn, November 26, 2019.

2. Jared Spataro, "2 Years of Digital Transformation in 2 Months," *Microsoft 365* blog, April 30, 2020, https://www.microsoft.com/en-us/microsoft-365/ blog/2020/04/30/2-years-digital-transformation-2-months/. Accessed July 13, 2020.

3. "Introduction," *2020 Deloitte Global Human Capital Trends: The Social Enterprise at Work: Paradox as a Path Forward*, p. 13.

4. "Connecting to Purpose," Deloitte *WorkWell* podcast, https://www2.deloitte .com/us/en/pages/about-deloitte/articles/workwell-podcast-series.html. Accessed June 10, 2020.

5. Gerald C. Kane, Anh Nguyen Phillips, Jonathan R. Copulsky, and Garth R. Andrus, *The Technology Fallacy: How People Are the Real Key to Digital Transformation*, Cambridge, MA: MIT Press, 2019, p. 33.

6. Emma Seppälä, "Positive Teams Are More Productive," *Harvard Business Review*, March 18, 2015, p. 3.

7. "Edison's Lightbulb," The Franklin Institute, https://www.fi.edu/history -resources/edisons-lightbulb. Accessed July 13, 2020.

8. "Putting People First: Successful Digital Is Less About the Tech Than You Think," *Wired Insider*, Deloitte Digital, 2019, https://www.wired.com/wired insider/2019/10/putting-people-first-successful-digital-transformation-less -tech-think/. Accessed April 20, 2020.

9. An example provided by the SixSigma Institute: 3.4 defects per 1 million opportunities for a defect, https://www.sixsigma-institute.org/What_Is_Sigma_And_ Why_Is_It_Six_Sigma.php. Accessed July 15, 2020.

10. Emiliya Zhivotovskaya, with Jen Fisher, "Bouncing Back," Deloitte *WorkWell* podcast, https://www2.deloitte.com/us/en/pages/about-deloitte/articles/ workwell-podcast-series.html. Accessed June 10, 2020. Emiliya Zhivotovskaya is CEO of The Flourishing Center.

11. Sam Harnett, "Cities Made Millions Selling Taxi Medallions, Now Drivers Are Paying the Price," NPR, October 15, 2018.

12. "What Is Designing Thinking?," *IDEO U* blog, https://www.ideou.com/blogs/ inspiration. Accessed July 18, 2020.

Chapter 4

1. Kim Christfort and Suzanne Vickberg, *Business Chemistry: Practical Magic for Crafting Powerful Work Relationships*, Hoboken, NJ: Wiley, 2018.

2. Ibid., p. 8.

3. See Susan Cain's excellent book *Quiet: The Power of Introverts in a World That Can't Stop Talking*, New York: Crown Publishers, 2012.

4. Bruce Anderson, "5 'Ridiculous' Ways Patagonia Has Built a Culture That Does Well and Does Good," LinkedIn, September 27, 2019.

5. Larry Emond, "Sanofi CHRO: Culture and Identity Are Two Different Things. A Conversation with Roberto Pucci," Gallup, May 10, 2018.

6. Arthur C. Brooks, "The Three Equations for a Happy Life, Even During a Pandemic," *The Atlantic*, April 9, 2020.

7. "Designing Work for Well-Being: Living and Performing at Your Best," *2020 Deloitte Global Human Capital Trends—The Social Enterprise at Work: Paradox as a Path Forward*, p. 37.

8. "Well-Being: A Strategy and a Responsibility," *2018 Deloitte Global Human Capital Trends—The Rise of the Social Enterprise*, pp. 67–68.

9. Eric Mosley and Derek Irvine, *Making Work Human: How Human-Centered Companies Are Changing the Future of Work and the World*, New York: McGraw Hill, 2020, p. 198.

Chapter 5

1. "Introduction," *2020 Deloitte Global Human Capital Trends—The Social Enterprise at Work: Paradox as a Path Forward*, p. 13.

2. "Belonging: From Comfort to Connection to Contribution," *2020 Deloitte Global Human Capital Trends*, pp. 27 *ff*.

3. "Opossum: *Didelphis virginiana*," San Diego Zoo, https://animals.sandiegozoo .org/animals/opossum. Accessed August 10, 2020.

4. Brené Brown, *The Gifts of Imperfection: 10th Anniversary Edition*, New York: Random House, 2020. p. 37.

5. Maria Konnikova, "The Limits of Friendship," *New Yorker*, October 7, 2014, https://www.newyorker.com/science/maria-konnikova/social-media-affect -math-dunbar-number-friendships. Accessed August 20, 2020.

6. Laura-Kristine Krause and Jérémie Gagné, Fault Lines: Germany's Invisible Divides, More in Common, 2019; Tim Dixon, "Here's How We Solve the Global Crisis of Tribalism and Democratic Decay," *World Economic Forum*, January 9, 2019.

7. "Belonging: From Comfort to Connection to Contribution," *2020 Deloitte Global Human Capital Trends*, p. 26.

8. Jake Herway, "How to Bring Out the Best in Your People and Company," Gallup Workplace, March 6, 2018, https://www.gallup.com/workplace/232958/bring -best-people-company.aspx. Accessed April 22, 2020.

9. Alison Beard, "True Friends at Work," *Harvard Business Review*, July–August 2020, p. 138.

10. "The Value of Belonging at Work: New Frontiers for Inclusion," BetterUp, 2019, p. 7.

11. Annamarie Mann, "Why We Need Best Friends at Work," Gallup, January 15, 2018.

12. Naz Beheshti, "10 Timely Statistics About the Connection Between Employee Engagement and Wellness," *Forbes* online, January 16, 2019.

13. Kim Cameron, Carlos Mora, Trevor Leutscher, and Margaret Marie Calarco "Effects of Positive Practices on Organizational Effectiveness," *Journal of Applied Behavioral Science*, vol. 47, no. 3, pp. 266–308, January 26, 2011.

14. Jim Purcell, "Employee Well-Being: A New Perspective on ROI," *Forbes*, February 11, 2020.

15. "Workplace Well-Being Linked to Senior Leadership Support, New Survey Finds," American Psychological Association, June 1, 2016.

16. "Win with Empathy: Global Talent Trends 2020," Mercer, p. 51.

17. Jim Guszcza and Jeff Schwartz, "Superminds: How Humans and Machines Can Work Together," *Deloitte Review*, no. 24, January 28, 2019.

18. Ibid.

19. Dacher Keltner, "Science of Emotions," Deloitte *WorkWell* podcast, https:// www2.deloitte.com/us/en/pages/about-deloitte/articles/workwell-podcast -series.html. Accessed June 10, 2020.

20. Ibid.

21. "Understanding Acute and Chronic Inflammation," *Harvard Men's Health Watch*, April 2020, https://www.health.harvard.edu/staying-healthy/understanding -acute-and-chronic-inflammation. Accessed August 25, 2020.

Chapter 6

1. Vivek Murthy, "Work and the Loneliness Epidemic: Reducing Isolation at Work Is Good for Business," *Harvard Business Review*, September 2017, https://hbr.org/cover-story/2017/09/work-and-the-loneliness-epidemic. Accessed August 31, 2020.
2. *Deloitte Tech Trends 2020.*
3. "Deloitte Digital's Amelia Dunlop on Elevating the Human Experience," Ad Age Studio 30, December 28, 2020.
4. Jake Herway, "How to Bring Out the Best in Your People and Company," Gallup Workplace, March 6, 2018, https://www.gallup.com/workplace/232958/bring-best-people-company.aspx. Accessed April 22, 2020.
5. Dacher Keltner, "Science of Emotions," Deloitte *WorkWell* podcast, https://www2.deloitte.com/us/en/pages/about-deloitte/articles/workwell-podcast-series.html. Accessed June 10, 2020.
6. Larry Emond, "Sanofi CHRO: Culture and Identity Are Two Different Things. A Conversation with Roberto Pucci," Gallup, May 10, 2018.
7. David Burkus, "How to Tell if Your Company Has a Creative Culture," *Harvard Business Review*, December 2, 2014, https://hbr.org/2014/12/how-to-tell-if-your-company-has-a-creative-culture. Accessed September 4, 2020.
8. Emma Seppälä, "Organizational Culture: Positive Teams Are More Productive," *Harvard Business Review*, March 18, 2015.
9. Tracy Brower, "5 Predictions About How the Coronavirus Will Change the Future of Work," *Forbes* online, April 6, 2020.

Chapter 7

1. "Well-Being: A Strategy and a Responsibility," *2018 Deloitte Global Human Capital Trends: The Rise of the Social Enterprise*, pp. 65–70.
2. *2020 Deloitte Global Human Capital Trends—The Social Enterprise at Work: Paradox as a Path Forward.*
3. Andrew T. Jebb, Louis Tay, Ed Diener, and Shigehiro Oishi, Happiness, Income Satiation and Turning Points Around the World," *Nature Human Behaviour*, vol. 2, pp. 33–38, 2018, https://doi.org/10.1038/s41562-017-0277-0.
4. Workplace Burnout Survey: Burnout Without Borders, Deloitte 2015 external workplace well-being survey.
5. Kelly Monahan, Mark J. Cotteleer, and Jen Fisher, "Does Scarcity Make You Dumb? A Behavioral Understanding of How Scarcity Diminishes Our Decision Making and Control," Deloitte University Press, 2016.
6. Ibid., p. 12.
7. "Creating and Practicing Healthy Habits," Deloitte *WorkWell* podcast, Special COVID-19 edition, Episode #4, https://www2.deloitte.com/us/en/pages/about-deloitte/articles/workwell-podcast-series.html. Accessed June 10, 2020.
8. "Benefits of Sleep," Division of Sleep Medicine at Harvard Medical School, http://healthysleep.med.harvard.edu/healthy/matters/benefits-of-sleep. Accessed September 28, 2020.

9. "How Much Sleep Do I Need?," Centers for Disease Control and Prevention, https://www.cdc.gov/sleep/about_sleep/how_much_sleep.html. Accessed January 21, 2021.

10. Suzanne Bertisch, "Strategies to Promote Better Sleep in These Uncertain Times," *Harvard Health Blog, March 27, 2020.*

11. Gerald C. Kane, Rich Nanda, Anh Nguyen Phillips, and Jonathan R. Copulsky, *The Transformation Myth: Leading Your Organization Through Uncertain Times,* Cambridge, MA: MIT Press, September 2021.

12. Willem Christiaan van Manen, Fleurine Mijinke, and Ties Hamers, "Impact of COVID-19 on the Hospitality Industry," Report, Deloitte Netherlands.

13. Maria Konnikova, "What Makes People Feel Upbeat at Work," *New Yorker,* July 30, 2016.

14. Jen Fisher, "The Thrive Guide to Safeguarding Your Mental Health in the Time of COVID-19," Thrive Global, April 23, 2020, https://thriveglobal.com/stories/coronavirus-crisis-toll-on-mental-health-solutions/. Accessed September 29, 2020.

Chapter 8

1. "Understanding Emotional Agility," Deloitte *WorkWell* podcast, October 15, 2020.

2. "The Future of Jobs," World Economic Forum, January 2016, p. 22.

3. Marina Krakovsky, "Why Mindset Matters," *Stanford Magazine,* September 20, 2017.

4. Jen Fisher, "The Thrive Guide to Managing Emotions at Work," Thrive Global, November 20, 2020. https://thriveglobal.com/stories/how-to-manage-emotions-in-the-workplace-2/. Accessed March 29, 2021.

5. "Understanding Emotional Agility."

6. Susan Cain, *Quiet: The Power of Introverts in a World That Can't Stop Talking,* New York: Crown Publishers, 2012, pp. 1–15.

7. Adam Grant, Twitter post, October 9, 2020.

8. Rasmus Hougaard, "Four Reasons Why Compassion Is Better for Humanity Than Empathy," *Forbes,* July 8, 2020.

9. Kate Murphy, "We're All Socially Awkward Now," *New York Times,* September 1, 2020.

10. Betsy Mikel, "How Brené Brown Runs Emotionally Intelligent Zoom Meetings." Inc. April 15, 2020.

Chapter 9

1. *The Social Dilemma,* Netflix documentary. Accessed October 16, 2020.

2. World Bank, World Development Indicators. Our World in Data, https://ourworldindata.org/technology-adoption#mobile-money-account-adoption. Accessed December 9, 2020.

3. Manfred E. Clynes and Nathan S. Kline, "Cyborgs and Space," *Astronautics,* September 1960, p. 26.

4. Alan Lightman, *Searching for Stars on an Island in Maine*, New York: Pantheon, 2018, p. 194.

5. "Taming Technology," Deloitte *Workwell* podcast, https://www2.deloitte.com/us/en/pages/about-deloitte/articles/workwell-podcast-series.html. Accessed June 10, 2020.

6. "The Future of Work," MIT Initiative on the Digital Economy, July 2018.

7. Laura Silver, "Smartphone Ownership Is Growing Rapidly Around the World, but Not Always Equally," Pew Research Center, February 5, 2019.

8. J. Clement, "Facebook: Number of Monthly Active Users Worldwide 2008–2020," Statista, August 10, 2020.

9. "Winning," Deloitte SpokenCinema #H264 2019.

10. "Taming Technology."

11. Ibid.

12. Jean M. Twenge, "The Sad State of Happiness in the United States and the Role of Digital Media," *World Happiness Report 2019*. This report focuses on adolescent research, and Twenge suggests the trends are similar for adults. See also Twenge, "Why Increases in Adolescent Depression May Be Linked to the Technological Environment," *Current Opinion in Psychology*, April 2020, pp. 89–94.

13. "Positive Technology: Designing Work Environments for Digital Well-Being," Deloitte Insights report, 2018.

14. Ibid.

15. Amy Blankson, "Good Tech," Deloitte *WorkWell* podcast, https://www2.deloitte.com/us/en/pages/about-deloitte/articles/workwell-podcast-series.html. Accessed June 10, 2020.

16. Emiliya Zhivotovskaya, "Bouncing Back," Deloitte *WorkWell* podcast, https://www2.deloitte.com/us/en/pages/about-deloitte/articles/workwell-podcast-series.html. Accessed June 10, 2020.

17. Charles Duhigg video on the power of habit, https://charlesduhigg.com/the-power-of-habit/. Accessed October 22, 2020.

18. Two activities can operate concurrently if one is unconscious. For example, you can walk and talk at the same time because most of the time the walking is directed unconsciously. But the moment you trip or you realize you are lost, your attention shifts instantly to your surroundings.

19. "Taming Technology."

20. "Fareed Zakaria's Guide to a Post-Pandemic Age," *Innovation Hub* podcast, October 23, 2020.

21. "Zoom and Gloom: The Transition to Remote Work Is Welcome. But It Will Be Painful," *The Economist*, October 8, 2020.

22. Ethan Bernstein and Ben Waber, "The Truth About Open Offices," *Harvard Business Review*, November–December 2019.

23. Gensler U.S. Work from Home Survey 2020, Briefing #1, https://www.gensler.com/research-insight/blog/insights-from-genslers-u-s-work-from-home-survey-2020?o=boston. Accessed December 9, 2020.

Chapter 10

1. "Well-Being: A Strategy and a Responsibility," *2018 Deloitte Global Human Capital Trends—The Rise of the Social Enterprise*, p. 69.
2. Nereida Moreno, "Chicago Distillery Pivots to Supply Hand Sanitizer During COVID-19," WBEZ Chicago, April 24, 2020.
3. Samantha Pell, "A Sports Company Started Making Medical Gear Instead of Hockey Visors. It Wants Others to Help," *Washington Post*, March 28, 2020.
4. Peter Valdes-Dapena, "Automakers Are Still Cranking Out Masks and Other PPE as Covid Roars Back," CNN Business, December 8, 2020.
5. "How to Support Mental Health at Every Level of Your Organization," Quartz live workshop, October 29, 2020.
6. Ibid.
7. Susan David, "Understanding Emotional Agility," Deloitte *WorkWell* podcast, October 2020. David is the author of *Emotional Agility: Get Unstuck, Embrace Change and Thrive in Work and Life.*
8. Kelly Greenwood, Vivek Bapat, and Mike Maughan, "Research: People Want Their Employers to Talk About Mental Health," *Harvard Business Review*, November 22, 2019.
9. George Anders. "Sleeping with Your Smartphone? Here's the Cure," *Forbes* online, May 17, 2012.
10. "Time Off with John Fitch and Max Frenzel," Deloitte *WorkWell* podcast, October 2020. Fitch and Frenzel are the authors of *Time Off: A Practical Guide to Building Your Rest Ethic and Finding Success Without the Stress.*
11. Framework adapted from Jen Fisher, "Designing Work for Well-Being," from *2021 Deloitte Global Human Capital Trends—The Social Enterprise in a World Disrupted: Leading the Shift from Survive to Thrive.*
12. In the documentary *The Social Dilemma,* the inventor of Facebook's "Like" button says with regret that he never thought an expression of approval between friends would become an object of obsession, as in "How many likes did I get today?"

Conclusion

1. *Success Made to Last* podcast, October 9, 2020.
2. Adapted from Jen Fisher, "How to Be the Chief Well-Being Officer of Your Own Life," Thrive Global, October 21, 2020. https://thriveglobal.com/stories/chief-well-being-officer-life-lessons-leadership-goals-stress/. Accessed March 29, 2021.

INDEX

ABOUT THE AUTHORS

Jen Fisher is a leading voice on workplace well-being and the creation of human-centered organizational cultures. She frequently speaks and writes about building a culture of well-being at work and hosts *WorkWell*, a podcast series on the latest work-life trends. Jen currently serves as Deloitte's chief well-being officer in the United States, where she drives the strategy and innovation around work-life, health, and wellness. In her role, she empowers Deloitte's people to prioritize their well-being so they can be at their best in both their professional and personal lives. Jen is a healthy lifestyle enthusiast and seeks to infuse aspects of wellness in everything she does. She believes self-care is a daily pursuit and considers herself an exercise fanatic, sleep advocate, and book nerd! As a breast cancer survivor, she is passionate about advocating for women's health and sharing her recovery journey. Jen lives in Miami with her husband, Albert, and dog, Fiona.

Anh Phillips has dedicated her career to exploring the interplay between technology and humanity. She is coauthor of *The Technology Fallacy*, a data-driven look at the centrality of culture to digital transformation. Her work has been cited in leading publications such as the *Wall Street Journal*, *MIT Sloan Management Review*, *Forbes*, *Fortune*, and *CIO Magazine*. A senior leader at Deloitte Consulting, Anh directs research teams that help the C-suite and board focus on the important role that technology, leadership, and culture play in fostering innovation. When Anh isn't writing books, she's reading books. She occasionally takes breaks to cook and travel with her husband, John, and two kids, Sophie and Julian. They call Atlanta home.